If not now, when?

HEAL YOUR HEALTH
Nourishing Your Mind, Body and Spirit Naturally

Dr. Stacey Cooper
B.Sc. (H.K.), D.C.

Also By Dr. Stacey Cooper

Dr. Stacey Cooper's Healthy Fuels Cookbook™
Fuelling Your Body For Enhanced Vitality Naturally
Wheat, Gluten, Dairy, Soy and Sugar Free Recipes
that your whole family will love

International Bestseller
What's Self-Love Got To Do With It?
How 14 women learned to love themselves.
Compiled with Heather Andrews

25 AWESOME PEOPLE I KNOW
with Sarah Pass and Friends

HEAL YOUR HEALTH
Nourishing Your Mind, Body and Spirit Naturally

Dr. Stacey Cooper
B.Sc. (H.K.), D.C.

10-10-10
Publishing

Heal Your Health - Nourishing Your Mind, Body and Spirit Naturally
Second Edition June 2019
www.DrStacey360.com
Copyright © 2019 Dr. Stacey Cooper
ISBN: 978-1-77277-264-7

Publisher
10-10-10 Publishing
Markham, ON Canada

Printed in Canada and the United States of America

Table of Contents

December 12, 2019
Brantford, ON.

Dear Julie

This book I dedicate to you!
The innate power within you is your true gift
to use and to choose differently.
Choosing differently creates different outcomes,
and I thank you for choosing me to walk with you on your
path to Healing Your Health Naturally.

If not now, when?

Sincerely
Dr Stacey.

Foreword

It is my full intention to live a vibrant life in abundant health to the age of 120. You may think that this is impossible, but I have come to understand that the body is a remarkable healing mechanism. I am continuously learning of natural and wholistic ways to support my body in order to accomplish this.

After reading this book, you too will be empowered, as I was, with the understanding of the healing capacity that you have available to you during every single moment of your life. You will marvel at how simple it is to retake control over all aspects of your life. I read this book very carefully, taking notes as I went along, largely because I have so much respect for the woman who created it. I can say with certainty that the contents of this book have brought me to a whole new awareness of what I can do for myself, in order to avoid the efforts of the many external factors in today's society which seem to conspire in keeping me from living my life at the level of optimal health that I desire.

It is so unfortunate to find yourself in such a state, in this day and age, where you are always looking outside of your perfect self, searching for solutions and at the same time ignoring your own healing potential which is found within. My friend Dr. Stacey Cooper has provided, for you, a wholistic guide for reversing this trend, to lead you on the journey to self-healing. I recommend you read this book with a pen in hand as you will want to make notes in the margins and return to these illuminating insights that are designed to make your life infinitely better.

Dr. Stacey shares that health does not just come from the foods that you eat, and she also shares her physiological insight as to why diets do not work. This was such a relief to me. It was so refreshing to learn that weight loss can be effortless when you begin to support your body in the way it was designed, and that no diets are needed. Nourishing all aspects of your life is truly the key to obtaining optimal health, as Dr. Stacey shares with you here. Dr. Stacey's easy-to-read style, along with the life lessons that she shares throughout the book, really make this an enjoyable journey to a healthier lifestyle.

As you read and study the contents of this remarkable book, keep in mind that every choice you have is your choice to make. It truly is you who is in charge of every aspect of your life, including your health. I urge you to follow the Healthy Eating Blueprint™ that Dr. Stacey offers, and observe the transformation that you will experience by making the shift and healing your health naturally.

If you have found your way to Dr. Stacey, perhaps even "accidentally," you are well on your way to living a life with greater health. Dr. Stacey teaches by example, and lives what she teaches.

I love this book and I love the woman who created it. Read this book now, apply Dr. Stacey's ideas, and you will be grateful for all the wisdom that she reveals to you.

Raymond Aaron
New York Times Bestselling Author

Acknowledgements

Firstly to my husband **Dean Latimer** who has been by my side since we were 18 years old. Without you none of this would be possible, for it was you who always believed in me more than I did. It was you who gave me the push and said "You need to do this. This is your calling and people are hungry for your message." Thank you for walking this road with me.

To our four incredibly talented children **Lyndsay**, **Kayla**, **Derek** and **Jake**. You have given me the gifts of perseverance, persistence, laughter and love, and have taught me countless lessons along the way. Thank you so much for being my teachers. I am so proud of you and I love you with all of my heart.

To my mother **Dianne Cooper**, I thank you for raising and nurturing me and always being there and supporting me through all of my adventures. I would not have been able to achieve all of my successes without you. To my brothers **Jayson** and **Tyler** for helping to shape me into the person I am.

To my in-laws **Kathy and Paul Latimer** for welcoming me into their family from the very beginning, and for their unwavering love and support through all of life's events.

To my two sisters-in-law and their families **Jenn**, **Gerald** and **Tanner** and **Lesley**, **Al**, **Jacob**, **Alethea**, **Degan** and **Tayden**. Life is so much fun with all of you in it!

To those who are no longer here but are forever with me and guiding me, my dad **Dr. Barry Cooper** for showing me the gift of healing that we all possess when our innate intelligence flows freely. To my namesake **Anastasia Laitar**, my baba, for sharing with me during her 93 years a life of grace and gratitude and just as she taught me I do learn something new each and every day. To my friend **Jill Robinson** who I shared a lifetime with in just the course of nine months. I too am delighted our paths have crossed. Thank you for teaching me how to soar.

To my dear friend **Rosemary Lee** who is also my cheerleader, my yoga instructor, my guide, my proofreader, my right arm and so much more. Thank you for enabling me to see all that I am to be in this lifetime.

To my business partner **Dr. Darrell Dailey**, your unwavering support and encouragement for me to follow my dreams is more than I can ever thank you for.

To our office assistants **Melanie**, **Rosemary**, and **Terri**. There has never been a task too big or too small that you haven't been able to step in to. Without each of you this book would never have come to completion. I thank you.

To my business mentors and my very dear friends **Noah and Babette St. John**. You were instrumental on that fateful day of April 4 2014 in expanding my vision to something in this world that I had never even considered, or let myself imagine, and yes Noah "You are right!" I am an author, and so much more.

To **Steve Robinson** and **Art Meade** for your friendship, which I hold so dear, and your continuous love and support. I thank Jilly Bean every day for bringing us together.

To my friend and accountability partner **Lynn Rossi**, thank you for your support as we bring the vision of our lives into this reality knowing that everything is possible.

To my friends **Elizabeth Moore**, **Danielle Sennhauser-Hughes**, and **Marcia Budd-Schnepf**. It is a joy working with you, and I thank you for your support.

To my dear friend, neighbour, classmate, and fellow horse lover **Nicole McGlogan**, thank you for always being there to lend an ear.

To my colleague and soul sister **Dr. Dena Churchill** for always being able to pick up right where we left off no matter how much time has passed.

To **Ra'eesa Baksh** and **Ali Baksh**, a remarkable sister and brother duo with incredible minds, powerful messages and tremendous talent.

I thank you for your continued support and for your dedication to making our world a better place for everyone in it.

To all of the members of our Empowered Women's Circle and to our wellness leaders **Dr. Catherine White Hansen, Carolina Batres, Marcia Way-Eng, Amy Gernaat,** and **Migdalia Hernandez**. I thank each of you for being on this journey with me and for your support as we lift each other through this community.

To my Balanced Living Academy™ members, **Joanne** and **Crystina, Vicki** and **Barry, Lin** and **Bob, Sharon** and **Wayne, Jean** and **Bob, Alanna, Yvonne** and **Ronnie, Karina** and **Tricia, Suzanne, Sheilagh, Simone, Joanne, Karen, Tammy, Lorie, Susan, Tiffany** and **Bruce, Kelly, Joan, Donna, Barb, Dianne, Sandy** and **Herb, Linda** and **Katherine, Susanne, Trish, Fern,** and **Susan**. I thank you for stepping into your new you as you enjoy a life filled with better body function and enhanced vitality.

To **Jenn Williams**, my stylist **Erin Putkowski,** and my clothier **Kristie Jordan** of Nina Brie, for enabling my true light to shine brightly.

To my Yaya's **Rosemary, Lynn, Bonnie, Tammy, Mari Lynne, Melanie, Mary, Paula,** and **Catherine**. The universe is truly abundant and ready for you to reach out and take hold. Thank you for seeing me through to my vision.

To my teachers and mentors. Expanding my mind and knowledge during this lifetime has made my life so much more fun and I thank you for sharing your gifts with me.

Dr. Fab Mancini (The Power of Self-Healing), **Dr. John DeMartini** (The Heart of Love), **Louise Hay** (You Can Heal Your Life), **Dr. Caldwell Esselstyn** and **Dr. T. Colin Campbell** (Forks Over Knives), **Dr. William Davis** (The Wheat Belly Book), **Deepak Chopra** (21-Day Meditation Experience), **Dr. Robert Holden** (Shift Happens), **Douglas Vermeeren** (Personal Power Mastery), **Jason Parker** (Olympic Medalist), **Antonina Bureacenco** (The Art of Wellbeing), **Jim Hetherington** (Relationship Breakthrough Specialist), **Lisa Berry** (International Radio Host -Light on Living), **Dr. Lana Marconi** (FiveD.TV), **Kelly Bentley** (Souely You Holistic Wellness), **Beth Bell** (International Radio Host -Beth Bell Radio Show on iHeart Radio), **Moira Bush** (TV Host -The Magenta Show), **Robert J.**

Moore (Robert J. Moore Inspires), **Sharon Staal** (Ladypreneurs Rising).

To my *What's Self-Love Got To Do With It?* co-authors **Heather Andrews**, **Nichole Jacobs**, **Corby Furrow**, **Nadine Hatzitolios McGill**, **Stefanie Davis Miller**, **Adele Desjardins-Lepine**, **Rosalyn Fung**, **Suzanne LaVoie**, **Alana Dixon-McAllister**, **Michelle Katherine Lee**, **Debra Salas**, **Shannon Watkins**, and **Carine Werner**. Thank you for being with me on my first journey into writing and lighting the fire within me.

To Raymond Aaron's team: **Layla, Aysha, Mikee, Liz, Christina, Danielle** and **Wendy** for your warm welcome, attention to every detail, and for making every event an experience to cherish.

To my Proctor Gallagher Institute Team: **DP Gates**, **Gina Hayden**, **Deborah Marnell**, and **Kathy Gallagher** for all of your support, guidance and encouragement as I continue to imagine, envision, and create my best life.

To **Cora Cristobal**, Founder of Toronto Women's Club, and **Lucy Jeffrey**, President of The Entrepreneur Nation, for your inspiration, drive, and desire to create such incredible communities.

To **Mark Stephen Pooler** for helping me to share my message globally.

To **Satish Verma**, CEO of the Think and Grow Rich Institute. I truly appreciate your support of my project as we heal our world together.

To **Bhante Saranapala**, the Urban Buddhist Monk. I thank you for welcoming me to be part of your mission to help Canada to become a more Mindful and Kindful Nation.

To those who made this physical book come to be: **Liz Ventrella,** my personal book architect, **Lisa Browning**, my editor and formatter, **Waqas Ahmed** for my gorgeous book cover design, my son **Jake Latimer** for my cover photo and my daughter **Kayla Latimer** for the illustrations.

To **Jack Canfield** for your dedicated presence. The first time we met you dubbed me "Dr. Healthy Fuels." The second time we met I had the opportunity to ask you, "What is your #1 non-negotiable health routine?" You proceeded to share the importance of meditation, exercise, consuming minimal sugar, having 8 hours of sleep per night, and your alkaline diet as being your non-negotiables. I thank you for affirming all that I share in this book. I am grateful for your book *The*

Success Principles and for your teachings at *The Canfield Training Group*. I now know that all I have to do is ASK in order to receive whatever it is that I imagine!

To **Bob Proctor** for your loving and generous heart and for taking the time, on the spot to help me hash out my title. Your words "Don't you know that more than 7 words on a billboard and no-one can read it?" will stay with me always. Thank you for introducing me to *Think And Grow Rich* and your teachings at the Proctor Gallagher Institute. I aspire to live my life as you teach, through my limitless imagination, with passion and a new found purpose. If not now, when?

To **Raymond Aaron**, my mentor, and publisher. For your incredible teachings, guidance, support and program which enabled me to actually create a book in a way that I never knew was possible. Thank you Raymond, I am now an award-winning author and so much more!

Praise for *Heal Your Health*

"Having studied the mind for more than 50 years, I can say with some certainty that Dr. Stacey's book, *Heal Your Health*, is right on the mark. Healing is an inside job but it takes on even greater power when your body is fuelled with what it needs to thrive. Mind is movement and your body is a manifestation of that movement. Your good health is waiting for you. What are you waiting for? Dive in and devour this book."
-Bob Proctor, Bestselling Author of *You Were Born Rich* and Teacher in *The Secret*

"Dr. Stacey's *Heal Your Health- Nourishing Your Mind, Body and Spirit Naturally* is a valuable key resource for balancing your life. I highly recommend it!"
-Jack Canfield, Coauthor of the *Chicken Soup for the Soul®* series and *The Success Principles™: How to Get from Where You Are to Where You Want to Be*

"Our world is in such need for what Dr. Stacey is sharing in *Heal Your Health*. In this book you will find inspiration as you gain the understanding of how your body functions and how to support it naturally, in order to experience optimal health. Dr. Stacey also provides great insight from her own journey here. I highly recommend this book."
-Satish Verma, President and CEO of Think and Grow Rich Institute

"As one of my coaching clients, Dr. Stacey has been one of my most consistent action-takers. Every time I showed her what to do, she went out and did it – which is why she got RESULTS! And one of the results is this remarkable book. I couldn't be more proud of the work Dr. Stacey has done or the person she is. And now you, the reader, get to reap the rewards in the form of better health and increased vitality. Enjoy this book and benefit from the wisdom it contains!"
- Noah St. John, The Power Habits® Mentor and Bestselling Author of *The Book of AFFORMATIONS®*

"This book is a must-read if you want to increase your health and well-being. Dr. Stacey writes from the heart and will inspire you to be the best you can be!"
- Babette St. John, Director of Noah St. John's Power Habits® Coach Network

"Dr. Stacey Cooper's ability to describe the inner workings of the human body is remarkable. With this knowledge along with her insight and the easy to implement steps that she provides, *Heal Your Health* is a must have resource for bringing balance into your life."
- Antonina Bureacenco, CNP, OHP

"If you would like to know how to live in a state of wellness and are seeking help then you've picked up the right book to guide you and support your growth. In these thoughtfully written chapters Dr. Stacey Cooper gives you practical tools and worthwhile information to cultivate the alignment of your mind and body for optimal health. Furthermore, her testimony to her own journey of well-being serves as a beacon of light to anyone desiring, initiating, and sustaining positive change."
-Lana Marconi, Ph.D., Award-Winning Documentary Filmmaker and Founder of FiveD.TV

"Dr. Stacey Cooper's love for life shines through in her story and her dedication to making her 'second chance' count is evident here in *Heal Your Health*. As an interviewer I have had the pleasure of working with Dr. Stacey and with my background and expertise in holistic nutrition and complete wellness I can say that Dr. Stacey is on the mark with the information she shares here. I highly recommend it. You will feel as if you have someone right beside you as you step into wellness."
-Lisa Berry, International Show Host, Author, Holistic Nutritionist and Life Coach

"I don't think there is a more relevant, or important topic today than the message Dr. Stacey Cooper is sharing in *Heal Your Health*. Today, perhaps more than ever, getting back to a place where there is complete balance in every facet of your life and being is a goal to be achieved. In my opinion I don't think there is a better person than Dr. Stacey to share this message. Her passion for overall health is evident. She lights up when she speaks about physical, mental, emotional and spiritual health and it comes through in her writing as well. This is a must read. The message is clear and I know that everything that she shares comes from her heart and from her wealth of experience, having tested and lived the principles herself."
-Jim Hetherington, International Award Winning #1 Bestselling Author, International Speaker, Teacher, Coach and Consultant

Chapter 1

Optimal Health

Health is the state of
optimal social, mental, and physical well being and
not merely the absence of disease or infirmity.
—World Health Organization

1-What Is It?

Health means so many different things to different people, but a common denominator that I have found is that without your health, what is there? This has become more and more evident over the course of my 22 years in practice as well as having suffered my own health crisis.

The biggest lesson that I learned from my crisis is that there is no price tag that I can put on my optimal health as it is truly priceless for me. The other lesson I learned is that if I don't take care of myself no one else is going to do it for me.

My purpose in writing this book for you is to share with you that optimal health is not just about the food you eat and the diets you follow. I am here to share with you an understanding as to how your body functions on the inside and to teach you that what you fuel your mind, body and spirit with has huge ramifications as to how your body will function on the inside. At times I will compare the function of your body to that of an engine. I expect that you are familiar with the concept that an engine needs fuel in order to run. I also expect that you may know that if diesel fuel is put into a gasoline engine it will not work effectively or efficiently and it may not even work at all. I will refer back to this concept throughout this book as I share with you how fuelling your mind, body and spirit differently will lead you to be able to change your health outcomes and will enable you to enjoy optimal health naturally. I am here to share with you that it is possible to heal your body and heal your health simply by changing the environment you provide for your body, as long as it is in a positive fashion.

Balance is the key to better body function and enhanced vitality, and there is not just one secret to reclaiming your health. The food that you eat, the water that you drink, the exercise that you provide for your physical body, the meditation and stress reduction that you provide for your emotional being as well as your self-care routines, your relationships and your mindset are all vital to reclaiming your optimal health, and I am so excited to be sharing this journey with you.

My blessing is to teach my proven methods for living life with less stress, improved health and well-being, and increased quality of life. My mission is to help health conscious people just like you to elevate your health to the next level. I am here to help you to up-level your health and well-being in order to enjoy enhanced vitality, increased happiness and improved quality of life naturally.

You are in the right place if you are confused about how to get healthy. I am here to share with you that it is not difficult, once you have an understanding as to how your body functions on the inside. I will be sharing with you simple steps that you can implement right away to begin to fuel your body differently in order for your engine to begin working more effectively and efficiently. The result will feel like you are trading in an old clunker for a high performance sports car.

Are you ready to take this ride with me? Let's get started!!

One of the first concepts to know is that your body is a miraculous mechanism which is forever adapting to every single stimulus that you encounter through every single microsecond of every single day, whether you are conscious of it or not. Your body's only purpose is to continuously maintain a balance point called homeostasis. Homeostasis is achieved when all of the systems in your body are working together in harmony. This is not an easy feat as there are so many outside forces which can throw off the harmony that your body is trying to maintain. Stressors here include chemical, emotional, physical, nutritional, financial, relational, and spiritual, to name a few. Your body can adapt to a whole variety of things and it does the best it can with what you provide for it, but it does have a finite limit as to the amount of adaptation it can undergo. When your body reaches its limits of adaptation, its function begins to deteriorate, and signs and symptoms of disease processes begin to show up.

When you make a positive change in the environment that you are providing for your body, you can begin to heal your health naturally. I know this to be true because I have experienced both sides. It was not that long ago that I was in such a place in my life where I almost did not see the dawn of the next day. I am grateful for each and every day that I have, and because I was given a second chance I am making it count. I now dedicate my life to sharing how to achieve optimal health through nourishing your mind, body and spirit. I have studied, researched and gathered all kinds of information from a variety of sources, and have tried and tested many theories, programs, courses and systems. It has taken years but I now have developed the steps that I use for living a life with optimal health, and I am honoured to share some key strategies here with you. On the next page is a mind map for *Eliminating Your Hidden Energy Drainers*™.

I invite you to visit DrStaceyCooper.com where you can receive the accompanying FREE 2-part Video series and see how easy it is to begin to Eliminate your Hidden Energy Drainers™. You can receive this video training for free when you enter your name and email address on the site.

Now it is time to discover how easy it is to claim back your optimal health naturally.

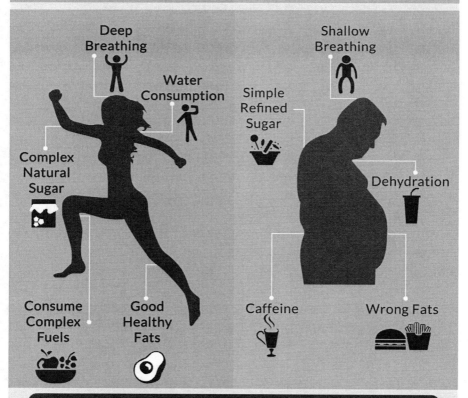

2-How Do You Obtain It?

The North American Society is in such a state health-wise that science now points to the fact that this is the first generation of children whose life expectancy is less than that of their parents. In general, throughout history life expectancy has always increased over time as society has witnessed improvements in living standards, increased cleanliness of water supplies, improved waste management systems and improved standards of sourcing food. Yet in the 21st century there is a shift in life expectancy and mortality rates, and this is not in a favourable direction as would be expected. It amazes me to find ourselves in this predicament even with all of the scientific advancements, gains in technology, and research. This decline in health is due in large part to the societal norm being that of instant gratification. Everything is expected to be available at the snap of a finger, and food delivery is no exception. Food preparation and food manufacturing practices have had to adapt to these expectations of the consumer and a result of this is the creation of food products that contain very little organic matter which enables it to have a longer shelf life and a shorter preparation time. This has not led to improved health. In fact the complete opposite is true. Also, the addition of chemicals, additives and preservatives leads to an increased toxic load on your system.

This is where you will find challenges to being healthy. Families where both parents work outside of the home, children with hectic social and recreational schedules, and the lack of "family sit-down mealtime" has all contributed to this epidemic due to the consumption of processed fast food. There is not enough time for you to exercise, or to make fresh homemade meals, and your schedule, at times, can just be too full.

Obesity, diabetes, heart disease, and high blood pressure are all diet related issues with exorbitant costs to the healthcare system each year. What may be surprising is that each of these health issues is a stand-alone issue. What that means is you do not have to be obese in order to have diabetes. You can have diabetes and not be obese. Cancer and diabetes are the two leading causes of death. I would like for you to take a moment and ponder this question: "How many people born today will develop diabetes in their lifetime?" Would you guess 1 in 20? Perhaps 1 in 10?

Studies show that one in three people born today will develop diabetes in their lifetime. This is outrageous! The good news is that this is reversible. The simple straightforward solution is to fuel your body well. If you severely limit or eliminate refined, processed, manufactured and animal based foods, you can prevent and even reverse some of the worst diseases. This can be accomplished by adopting a whole foods plant-based diet.

Now rest assured there are no vegan police. I am providing you with the scientific information as to how your body functions on the physiological level so that you can make informed choices as to what you provide for your body. The choice is yours. If you choose to fuel your body well for the majority of the time, feel free to splurge once in a while. But I caution you that once you start providing better fuels for your body and your engine begins to run more efficiently, it will not appreciate you putting in low-grade fuels, and those things that you had considered to be a treat may not go down as well once your body adapts to your new environment.

Proper fuel is essential to peak performance of any mechanism, and this includes your body.

If you put diesel fuel in a gasoline engine it will not run effectively or efficiently. Why would you expect anything different from your body?

3-Adaptation Of The Body

Your body is a remarkable adaptive mechanism, and this is the true essence of survival of the fittest. The sole purpose of your body is to maintain homeostasis. This is the balance point for all of the systems of your body. Your body will always do its best to adapt to the environment it finds itself in, whether that be a positive or negative environment. The catch is that there is a finite limit as to how much adaptation your body can do. I found this out first hand. The trick is to listen to your body. It does give warning signs when things are out of balance, and when you choose to not listen things can go awry quickly. When you choose not to listen to your body, it will shut you down and hit you over the head with a 2 x 4 in order to get your attention. This was my experience. I am certainly one of the lucky ones because I was given a second chance.

It is essential that your body adapts to the environment you are in. When the temperature outside is cold then your body will shiver in order to generate heat and keep you warm. This is a true survival mechanism. If it is too hot out then your body will create sweat in order to cool you down. This is your built in air-conditioning system. If you are faced with a danger or stress your body will shift its physiology in order to increase your heart rate and blood flow so that your physical being is ready to run away or fend off the perceived stressor. This is part of the fight and flight mechanism which is essential for survival.

You may be wondering what any of this has to do with the foods you eat. Your body was designed with its own chemistry lab built right in. You have enzymes, digestive secretions and hormones which are all utilized to digest the foods that you eat. The key factor here is that your body was designed to digest foods of the earth. The body is not equipped to break down things that were created in an artificial environment. When you consume foods that your body was not designed to utilize, this is when your engine is being fuelled with low octane fuels. Therefore your engine will run the best that it can with what is being provided, but it will not function optimally. It is known that if diesel fuel is put into a gasoline engine, that engine will not function well. The same thing is true for your body. Your body will adapt the best that it can, and it will utilize what is provided to the best of its ability, but it will not function optimally. Over the course of time, and if the body is not fuelled well, deterioration of the systems occurs, and signs and symptoms of disease processes begin to show up.

When you make the shift to change the environment that you provide for your body, including the fuels that you provide, your body can begin to adapt to this new environment, and healing is possible. It does not matter where you are starting from, what your age is, or what your goals are; each and every day is a new day. New choices can be made and you can begin providing a new environment for your body. As you begin to make this shift it will not take long for your body to notice. As you begin to make healthier choices in all areas of your life, you will begin to see how all aspects are interrelated. Nothing happens in isolation in the body. Your mental and emotional state affects how your body physically feels, and the foods you eat have direct effects on the energy levels that you experience. In order to experience optimal health it is essential to consider all aspects of your being — mental, emotional, spiritual, financial, physical, food choices, and relationships. When a shift is made in a positive direction in these areas of your life, your body will have an easier time achieving homeostasis, and will begin to experience improved function. With this comes a decrease of signs and symptoms of disease states as healing from within begins.

As the body receives the natural whole foods and the nutrients that it requires, its function begins to improve, and there is a shift in metabolism. This is when weight loss becomes effortless. As you continue on this journey in "Heal Your Health™" you will be able to experience first hand exactly what I am talking about.

4- You Are Not Tied To Your Genetics

As I move into the topic of healing your health, one of the most common oppositions I get is: "But Dr. Stacey, it is in my genes and there is nothing I can do about that."

So many of my patients and clients have expressed this concern, and they truly did fear for their health because they felt like there was no hope and that there was nothing that they could do proactively. I am here to tell you that this is far from the truth! I had one particular client share with me the following: "My mom died at the early age of 62 of heart disease. The medical doctor told us that it runs in the family. I am already on cholesterol medication and I have resigned myself to the fact that there is nothing that I can do. I have accepted the fact that this will be how I will die too." When I provided coaching to this client, their first reaction was that of relief. Finally they had found the tools to use to be able to take charge of their health outcomes and they were put back in control of their health. As they implemented the steps and tools I provided, they changed the environment they were providing for their body, and they have changed their health. They are no longer on cholesterol medication, they are happily exercising regularly, they have normalized their blood pressure and are able to out perform fellow employees who are half their age. They have also greatly reduced their stress levels as they no longer worry about their death sentence but are now enjoying their life to the fullest.

The information I am about to share with you here will shed new light on how you view your own DNA, and will give you hope that all is not lost. You will learn that just because Mom or Dad may have had a particular disease or condition does not mean that your outcome will be the same as theirs.

At this point it really doesn't matter which disease process you are speaking about; whether it be heart disease, cholesterol issues, diabetes, high blood pressure, arthritis, you name it, every single one of these conditions are degenerative disease processes. They are not genetic in nature. They all are a result of the body working to the best of its ability in a less than desirable environment. The good news is that because they are all degenerative in nature, they are all REVERSIBLE.

Science has shown that the signals from our genetic makeup can be turned on and off, depending on the environment that the body finds itself in. There is truth to the fact that certain conditions may run within families; however, this is tied more to the environment that is provided than just the genetics. The notion of "product of your environment" holds more weight here then strictly genetics. Generally within families, traditions, culture, and habits, are passed down through generations. When you provide the same environment for your body that your parents provided for their bodies, in general it is safe to say that you may experience the same outcomes as your parents. However, when you change your lifestyle habits in a positive direction, you are able to experience different outcomes than those of your parents because you are able to change your genetic expression based on the environment you provide for your body.

Just as I shared with you in the previous segment about adaptation of the body to its environment, your body is changing and adapting to every challenge and every stimulus during every single second of the day. Here is where you have a choice. You can choose to continue on the path you are on and have the same results, or you can choose to change. When you change in a positive direction the environment that you are providing for your body, and have your body adapt to the new environment, you will then be able to enjoy a different, positive outcome.

With this new-found information comes empowerment. Mental and emotional stress is greatly relieved when the sense of hopelessness is removed. Now you have the knowledge that you are not tied to your genetics and that you do have control over your outcomes. As you continue on your journey through the information provided here, and as you begin to implement ideas presented here, you will be able to experience a shift in your health and well-being. Initially the changes will be subtle, such as less gas and bloating, improved sleep patterns, and improved energy levels. As your body continues to adapt to your new environment you may experience enhanced digestion, improved moods, improved metabolism and effortless weight loss.

5-Healing From Within

The physiology of your body is designed in such a way that the digestive enzymes present within your digestive tract enable you to break down and utilize all of the building blocks from foods of the earth. However, in today's environment not all of your food comes from the earth. Your body does not have digestive enzymes to break down anything which was created in the laboratory, yet you may consume such ingredients in the form of additives, preservatives, sweeteners, artificial colours and flavours. When you consume these manufactured ingredients and chemicals, they are not broken down because you do not have the enzymes to do this and therefore they are not digested. They then accumulate in the blood purifying organs, the liver and kidneys, and over time can hinder the function of these organs, and your body can become toxic.

The fuels required for proper body function include water, fats, proteins, carbohydrates, vitamins, and minerals. All of these things come from the earth naturally. It is when you consume these components in an unbalanced fashion that your body then provides undesired results. This is one reason why diets do not work. The body requires all of these components in order to function optimally. When your diet is unbalanced then your body tries its best to adapt and cope with what is provided, but this will often lead to a shift in metabolism. Initially you may view this shift in a positive way; however, this is not sustainable, and is when your metabolism will stall, your body will plateau, and no further gains will be observed. This is because your body has gone into survival mode and it now will hold on to everything that you provide for it, thwarting your weight loss efforts.

Every single thing that you put in your mouth can either take you towards healing or away from it. As you become aware of how specific foods affect the function of your body it then becomes easier to make healthier choices. In Chapter 6 I will discuss what your body does with what you give it. When I share this information with my clients they tell me that they have never been taught this before and it has made all the difference to achieving success with their healthy living goals.

With the understanding of how your body is affected by the things that you eat, and when you want to achieve a specific health goal, your motivation is coming from within. When you know why a specific food takes you further away from achieving your goal, you are able to make choices which are in line with your commitment to obtaining your health goals.

Not all foods are created equal. All foods that you eat provide messages to your cells, tissues and organs. Some messages are positive and some are negative, just as some foods are inflammatory and some are healing. An unfortunate truth is that there are foods which we are told by the government and the mainstream media are good for you when in actual fact science shows that they actually cause degenerative disease processes in the body. So who are you to believe? That can be a tough call. I will be sharing information with you which I have thoroughly researched and which I implemented as I was on my own journey to regain my health. These are the same principles that I base my own health choices on to this very day. I shall lay it all out for you and then it is up to you to decide. There will be some things that you may already know. There may be some ideas that really resonate with you, and there may be others that you will sit and ponder for a while. Then there will be some that, at first, will go against everything that you thought to be true. I will ask you now to not simply dismiss the idea just because it is different from what you thought was true. It is said that if you want a different outcome then it is necessary to do things differently. I would instead ask you to at least entertain the idea, read what is presented, ponder it, critically research both sides of the issue and then at that point generate an informed opinion. I am simply here to share knowledge, cut through the propaganda and the advertising noise, and provide you with the physiological basis as to how your body works. You are in control of your outcomes and the steps you want to take in order to get there.

6- How These Principles Work In My Life

Life is a series of events that we react to either positively or negatively. How you respond to a stressor will create a shift in your energy. When you have the tools to be able to shift your response pattern, this will change your perceptions, and will then change your end result. When you are able to reduce the negative energy around you and approach life with gratitude, acceptance and thankfulness, every situation becomes more joyful, and I can tell you from experience that life is way more fun this way!

Here is just one story of how these life principles have helped me in my life. I was hosting my first ever live 2 day event, the Balanced Living Academy™. Despite all of the meticulous planning and preparation for my solo 2 day presentation, there were a few stumbling blocks placed in my path in the few days prior to the 8am start time on Friday morning.

Here is what happened. Wednesday morning at 11:30 I received a text from my caterer: "Please call me." As it turned out her cousin had passed in his sleep the night before, she wasn't sure when the funeral would be, she had the food bought for my event, hadn't cashed my deposit cheque and would understand if I wanted to go with someone else. She had made some of the food, but just wasn't sure how it was going to play out depending on what the funeral arrangements would be. WOW! I was so sorry for her loss and completely understood if she was not able to cater my event. On the other hand I really had no backup at all. When I was sourcing out a caterer for my Balanced Living Academy™, there were specific menu items that I required, and not just any caterer would do. I did not freak out. My life did not fall apart. As a problem solver, I would take on whatever needed to happen in order for the event to come together. Her short list of backups was quite short because everyone who she would have called on was in the family and they would be involved with the funeral. The first thing I did was text our daughter Kayla while she was at Canada's Wonderland with the high school junior band. I needed to ask her if she could move her scheduled driving lesson on Saturday afternoon in order to help us serve the lunch at the event. I asked her to give me a call from a quiet spot when she had a minute. I told her it was important but that it was not an emergency. When we talked she said "Yeah, sure Mom, I will text him right now and get my lesson moved." This immediately brought tears to my eyes. Not just tears of relief because she was able to help me, but because of the love and the lack of hesitation she had when I asked for help.

The next thing I did was start to write an email to my friends to send out feelers if they knew of anyone who could help serve a meal for us at the event. As I was doing that the caterer had texted me back and said that she had someone available for the Friday. I said, "Great, because I have Kayla for the Saturday." I did not hear from her for the rest of the day and it wasn't until well into the evening that she let me know that there would not be any conflicts with the scheduling for the weekend. Whew!

Now that is not the end of my story. At 8am on Thursday morning, I was in the parking lot of the grocery store as I just had a few things to pick up, and I received a text from my office assistant. Her ex-husband had passed away in his sleep that night and she was going to her daughter's house to wake her up and deliver the news to her daughter and 2 granddaughters. "WOW!" I took a deep breath. I did not freak out. What are you going to do? Stuff happens. I did have some things that I had planned for her to help me out with (so that I could be in 2 places at once) and now she was not going to be my right hand for the day as I had expected. I told her that she needed to look after herself and her family, and to not think about me or the office or anything else. So it was only me that was running the show at my office that day. I placed a note on the reception desk to let my patients know what was going on. They were all very patient, which was helpful.

The story does not end here. I was caring for my patients until 6 o'clock, and then our youngest son Jake had a soccer game so I took him to that. Our oldest boy Derek was reffing soccer and my husband Dean had work to get done because he was going to be spending 2 days supporting me at the event so he had to get ahead with his customers. My dear friend Nicole was helping me out to start getting set up on Thursday night, and as I was at Jake's game Nicole texted me. This was not good. She let me know that the parking lot where my event was being held was ripped up. It was going to be resurfaced and so was under construction. I laughingly replied "OK." What else could I do but laugh? This left me wondering what else could happen at this point. I said "Bring it on" as I was ready for anything now. I was thinking that things come in threes, but I threw that out the window because I said "What next?" There was nothing that was going to take me down. And as we began the event on Friday morning at 8am not any of my attendees had any inkling as to what I had been through the previous 36 hours. I know this because I shared this series of events with them at the end of the second day.

When stressors show up in your day, how do you tend to respond? Do you react positively or negatively? Do you let unexpected events ruin your day? Would you like to see the silver lining more often? If you would like to shift your perceptions and enjoy a life with less stress and have more fun, I invite you to check out the link BalancedLiving Academy.com and see how this can work for you too.

Through my experience and my crisis one thing that I have learned is that one of the first places to start in regards to decreasing stress levels in your life is to begin to show more love to yourself first. When you do this you will experience a huge shift in how you not only perceive your world around you in a more positive fashion, but also in how others will interact with you. I invite you to join me in the next chapter where I will share with you the importance of nourishing yourself with self-love.

But first I will ask you: "When, if not now?" This is what I have termed my W.I.N.N.'s. (**W**hen **I**f **N**ot **N**ow).

What W.I.N.N.'s have you thought about already from what you have learned so far? I have provided for you at the end of each chapter a full page for you to record your own W.I.N.N.'s. I encourage you to take time and reflect on what you have read, what ideas have resonated with you, and what has grabbed your attention. Be sure to hold on to that by capturing it and writing it down right now. You can jot down your biggest insights or realizations, set goals for yourself, and even copy down your favourite points from the chapter. It is simply a page at the end of every chapter that is dedicated to helping you organize your thoughts and realize your dreams.

When, if not now?

When, If Not Now?

Record Your W.I.N.N.s Here

_____

_____

_____

_____

_____

_____

_____

_____

_____

_____

_____

_____

_____

_____

_____

_____

_____

_____

_____

_____

_____

_____

_____

Chapter 2

Nourishing You

Disease cannot live in a body that is in a healthy emotional state.
—Bob Proctor

1-The Importance Of Self-love

Nourishing ourselves can come in many forms, but it has been my experience that not many people think of loving themselves when they think of nourishing themselves. Often the first thing that comes to mind in regard to nourishing yourself is the food you eat. But nourishing yourself wholistically includes so much more than just how you fuel your physical body with food. You are not just a physical being. There are so many more components to you that make you who you are.

Yes, it is true that the foods you eat are important in how you fuel your body, just as the quality of the air you breathe is important, and so is the purity of the water you drink. Each of these things is vital for your survival, but nourishing your mind and your spirit are also critical to your well-being. This has been shown over and over again when we examine the effects of solitary living on the human psyche and the well-being of a person. Humans are very social beings, and thrive when we have interactions with others and a sense of belonging within a community. When you come together with your peers who share similar interests, and show support towards one another, the impact of this has great effects on every aspect of your being, not only in regards to

17

emotional stability but also in regards to spiritual connection as well as improved health physically. Through my experience I have come to understand that self-love is the highest form of nourishment for your being.

It is unfortunate that it seems within our society that self-love can be looked upon as being selfish. As I was growing up, I was taught to always do for others, to put everyone else's needs ahead of my own and to sacrifice myself in the process. This notion can become so hardwired that it can become very difficult to change. I am here now to give you permission to make a shift as I did. Make a shift to love YOU. It has been said, and I believe, that if you do not love yourself first, no one else can love you. In order to love yourself, it is vitally important to know who you truly are, and this can only happen when you take the time to get quiet and listen to the voice within you, and become very familiar with what your heart truly desires.

I know for so many, and I include my past-self here as well, that schedules get so jam-packed and over-scheduled that there is no quiet time, no time for reflection, no time for listening to the inner voice. Oftentimes you may be so over-scheduled that you just keep running and running and never face what is in front of you. This is when you are running so fast that you are exhausted, doing for everyone else, and spreading yourself too thin.

In today's fast-paced world there never seems to be time to be quiet, to take time for yourself, unless you make that a priority. This is part of practicing self-love. When you begin to unload your schedule and actually make time so that you are able to catch your breath, even if just for a moment, it is truly amazing how quickly things can begin to shift and morph into a bright new you right before your eyes. All you have to do is get still, even just for a few minutes, and breathe and listen. At first this can be a scary task. Of course it is unknown territory for you, as it was for me, but rest assured that it does get easier. When you choose to make this shift in priority and actually begin to place yourself within your own schedule by incorporating "Me time" this will truly make a world of difference. During my Balanced Living Academy™ I witness the physical change within my attendees; how their physical being does a complete shift in energy and in posture with the realization that they are important, and that taking the time to make an effort to incorporate "Me time" into their day and allowing themselves to recharge their batteries is vital to their existence. This lifts a huge burden off their shoulders.

I highly encourage you to make this shift in mindset. When you choose to change your ways, that is when you see that practicing self-love actually enables you to give so much more to those around you. This is truly the greatest gift that you can give, not just to yourself, but to all of those in your life who you love.

2-Self-care Is Not Selfish

As I was growing up, I was always taught to be kind to those I met, to share my belongings with my friends, to give to others, and to not be selfish. These are a few of the ideals that I held on to for a very very long time. Being selfish is generally perceived in a negative light, and not as an honourable characteristic to possess. Here I would like to share with you what is considered the common definition of selfish. To be *selfish* is to lack consideration for others; to be concerned chiefly with one's own personal profit or pleasure. This ideal of not being selfish has been taught over and over from such an early age that it becomes a daily practice. Of course I did not question it because I was taught this by my parents and elders when I was a young child. I was also taught that parents know best, and to do as I was told and not ask questions. So of course I did believe that putting myself first was a selfish act. I really had no choice in the matter and at that age I did not have the resources or the thought patterns to question it. Belief systems are put in place before the age of 6 years old and can become engrained through repetition and time. This can make it very difficult for you to now shift from the ideals which you may have held on to for perhaps years, as this can be what you base your entire existence on. It can be very scary to make a shift from what you had believed to be a truth in your life. I am here to share with you right now that these ideas are completely false. As my past self I went to great lengths to do for others in order that others' opinions of me would be favourable. I would like you to take a moment now and I ask, can you feel the judgement right there from that previous statement? I know you always strive to do your best, and part of that comes from knowing that you will be judged by others. I had previously based my own self-worth on the opinions of others, and this had a direct impact on my feeling of being loved, and whether I felt I deserved to be loved.

This is no longer the case in my life. I cannot tell you how freeing it is to let go of judging others, and to not claim others' judgment of myself as truth. I have learned that, because everyone's perception of an event is based on their own life experiences and their life history, which does not include my life experiences, there is no such thing as a collective reality. The reason I can say this is because every single person has their own history and their own life experiences. It is how you react to your experiences, and then the learned behaviour which develops over the course of your lifetime, that creates your *perception* of the events around you at the present moment. The moments that you witness now become your own reality, which no one else has access to. And this is true for every single person. Every one of us has our own unique perception of the events that are experienced, thus no two of us are living in the same reality.

Now go back to the statement about being selfish. As stated, this is generally perceived in a negative light and not as an honourable characteristic to possess, and this was my belief as well. This is definitely something that I struggled with for a very long time. I am thrilled to say that I have been able to release it from my life. It was definitely a journey to come to this understanding and it does continue to be a work in progress, but I am here to tell you that it is doable and it is truly freeing of your spirit. Why is it that you spend so much time in judgement of yourself and of others? With my understanding now, to sit in judgement of myself or others is a waste of my valuable time and energy. I have come to place a much higher value on my time and my energy, and how I choose to use it, and this has also enabled me to let go of what I perceive to be everyone else's expectations of me. For I have come to the understanding in my heart that if I always strive to do my best and what I believe to be my best, I am the only one that I need to answer to, and there is no one else to please but myself. This realization did not come easily or quickly, but it did come when I took the time to be quiet with myself and to listen within and hear what my heart truly desires in this lifetime. This one concept alone has brought tremendous peace to my heart and soul.

As I said, this ideal of not being selfish was put upon me from the very beginning as a young person. When you stop and think for a moment about these traits, of course this is exactly the expected behaviour — to be kind, sharing and giving to others — and perhaps these are things that we continue to teach our children as well. The issue comes when you take this to the degree where you no longer consider yourself in the picture. When you spend so much time putting everyone else ahead of your own needs then there is very little, if any, time left over for you, and very little self-love is expressed.

3-No One Else Will Do It For You

When you do not take the time to practice self-love, many things result in the detriment of your health and well-being. I like to use the analogy of our bodies being like the engine of a car. Of course you know that when the car runs out of gas it will no longer run. You also know that if you do not maintain your car, if you do not change the oil, if you do not rotate the tires, if you do not maintain regular service, this is when the parts will start to wear out and the vehicle will become a hunk of junk in a very short period of time. The same is true for your body. When you do not take the time to recharge your batteries and replenish your fuel tank, this is when you become tired, frustrated, over-worked, stressed, miserable, exhausted, and your body does not have the opportunity to restore and replenish. This is when the systems begin to break down and disease processes ensue. This is when signs and symptoms began to show up and your health deteriorates. When you are living from a place of selflessness where you are always giving to others, and thinking about what is best for others as your first priority, as with everything that your being has to contend with, if that 'thing'

21

or stressor happens to draw you away from homeostasis, the balance point of the body, the systems in your body begin to break down.

As I will share with you throughout this book, your body is a remarkable adaptive mechanism. It is always adapting to the environment you provide for it. It does not matter if that environment is positive or negative, as your body will always adapt to the best of its ability. However, there is a finite limit to how much adaptation your body can accomplish. When such enormous demands are placed on your own personal resources and you do not take the time to replenish your reserves, the tank runs dry and your engine begins to break down.

As I was moving through the chapter in my life which led to my health crisis, of course it was not until after the fact that I realized that if you don't take care of yourself no one else is going to do it for you. It was during this time in my life that there was zero self-love being practiced, and this resulted in the loss of my health. Actually now when I reflect back on it I truly believe that I had no idea then what self-love even was. It was a time in my life where I was left in the rut of the patterns which I had developed due to what I had learned throughout my upbringing. I had taken on the expectations that others placed on me. The list of duties which I then piled onto myself became overwhelming because of course it was also my understanding that to ask for help was a sign of weakness. As I reflect back on this period I do believe that I may even have consciously over-scheduled my time in order to not have any extra time to think about the situation I was in, or to contemplate what my future might hold. For many this is a protective mechanism purely through avoidance. It certainly does not mean that the situation or stressors do not exist, it just means that you choose not to acknowledge them. Of course this is the "Ostrich Syndrome" where your head is buried in the sand. Rest assured that at some point you will need to come up for a breath of air, and when you lift your head out of the sand this is often when the freight train of life can hit you square between the eyes, seemingly without warning. This is where I found myself to be, and trust me, it is not a good place.

It truly is up to you to take back your power, and to take charge of all that you desire. No one else can make these choices for you. So I give you permission now to grab hold of the reins of your life, which may seem like it is charging ahead like a runaway freight train. Pull back on those reins and gain control. Doing exactly this is what saved my life, and gave me a second chance. Seize your chance right now. It is not too late, trust me.

For your own copy of "What's Self-Love Got To Do With It?" my E-Book version is available at https://drstaceycooper.com/self-love-book/ and enter Coupon Code: LOVE for 50% off, or to purchase the soft cover copy just email me at drstacey@drstaceycooper.com and I will provide free shipping.

When you take control and begin to exhibit self-care, this gives you the opportunity to recharge your batteries, reduce your stress, calm your mind and strengthen your body so that you may serve others to your greatest capacity. This then enables you to live a life you LOVE! Self-care is not selfish. You must look after yourself as no one else is going to do it for you.

4-Getting You On Your Own Priority List

A bold move forward here would be to actually get yourself onto your own priority list. Each day you know there are certain things that you *need* to accomplish, such as getting to work, perhaps delivering children to school, or attending to appointments etc. These are often your commitments or obligations. Then there are those things that you *want* to accomplish in your day, and some of those things may even be just for you and your own self-care. Often it is these items which are put at the bottom of the priority list, if they even make the list in the first place. It is my hope that you can see the difference between needs and wants in these two scenarios. Through conversation with many of my clients it is evident that often there is not enough time to allow for fulfilling all of the tasks on the day's priority list. When you run out of time in the day before you reach the end of the list, this is when the things which you *wanted* to do for yourself tend to get left hanging on the list. When the next day arrives, those things which did not get completed from the day before will often get moved to the list of the new day; however, they do not necessarily land at the top of the new list. What frequently happens is that the items get moved to the new list but the new list then gets re-prioritized. Thus your self-care ends up going by the wayside because your priority list is in perpetual motion and you seldom get to the tasks that you *want* to do because you may spend the majority of your time taking care of the tasks that you *need* to get done.

This is why I place such emphasis on scheduling. In this day and age so many of us are tied to our phone. How often do you notice that if an event or an appointment is not in your phone then it simply does not exist? The same is true for your self-care. If you have not scheduled your self-care then how do you expect it to show up in your day? If you have not scheduled your self-care then when will you work it into your already hectic day? I am here to give you permission to love yourself. To give you permission to take time within your own day just for you. When you make this shift in mindset and come to know that self-care is not selfish (contrary to what some societies dictate) you will begin to place yourself on your own priority list. To take this a step further is to put yourself at the top of your priority list.

When I share with my clients the CLEAN™ Living Formula I teach them the concept of hard and soft entries in the daily schedule. *Hard entries* are such things as your daily commitments. These are things which are not easily changeable. They are life commitments that you have, some of which may include your work schedule, your health and wellness appointments, your daily living chores such as grocery shopping, laundry, and paying bills. *Soft entries* are such things as perhaps a social gathering for work, going to the mall, or just passing time. When I speak of hard entries in your calendar I recommend that you "ink" them in, not pencil them in. This means that they are not erasable, they are not negotiable, and they are your first priorities.

Now you can see how easy it is to begin to implement time just for you. I teach clients to break this down into two steps. The first step is to identify some of the things which you would really enjoy doing just for you. This can definitely include things that you have always longed to do and just never made the time for. A few ideas may include taking a class, picking up a new hobby, learning a new craft, finding time to go to the gym or for a walk, or simply just taking time to read a good book. Whatever it is that you want to explore for yourself, I encourage you to just choose to do that.

The next step is now to actually schedule that activity into your day as a hard entry. Don't just have it as an idea, or that perhaps you might do it. I am here to give you permission to make it happen for you. The best way I know how to make it happen is to schedule it. Take the time now to go to your calendar and place your new activity in a time slot which is achievable. This is a critical factor in your success to see your "me time" and self-care come to fruition. The reason I say this is because if you schedule your activity into a time slot which is not doable, then just as the word implies, it won't get done. For instance, if I were to schedule my exercise time during the course of the day when I am commuting home from the office, of course I am not going to be able to make it happen. Be sure that you set up your "me time" in a time slot that works for you, and also be sure that the activity that you schedule for yourself is something that you actually want to do. If you schedule a 30 minute swim right after work on Tuesday at 4:30pm but you hate swimming, then of course your likelihood of completing this activity is extremely low. Perhaps a better activity might be to schedule a 20 minute run right after work on Tuesday at 4:30pm at the local running track. This is a solid commitment in my calendar and is something that I enjoy doing; it is convenient and on my way home, and it is free. All of these factors will dramatically increase my chance of success in accomplishing this task. I encourage you to make sure that, as you begin to prioritize your self-care and start taking care of you first, the tasks that you set out for yourself are achievable. This is one of the best ways to ensure your success.

5-Superheroes Do Not Exist

Now is the time that you can begin to unload your schedule. It may be frightening, but I ask you to take a look at your schedule and figure out how much of what is there is actually for other people. Take a moment to determine what percentage of your daily activities is actually for you. It may shock you. It shocked me to see how little time I was actually dedicating to myself in the days of my past. No wonder my wheels fell off and my life derailed. It was not until I reached this point that I knew that if I continued as I was I would be in serious trouble, and I would no longer be able to do anything at all. This is when I came to the realization that, contrary to popular belief, I do not have to be everything to everyone, and I do not need super human powers. I do not need to be a superhero, and I am not superhuman! I often felt in the past that I did need to be superwoman. I expect that I choose to tie my self-worth to my achievements. Here again is where judgement played a big part in my life. I was relying on the judgement of others to determine my belief in myself. For me this came from my ideals that achievement equals love, success comes from achievement, and it then follows that the more you achieve the greater your success. The unfortunate part is that this can result in the feeling of never being enough, which then just continues to fuel the endless cycle of feeding into the superhero complex. This is when you continue to cram your schedule so full and over-extend yourself to such a degree that you end up waking up in the morning with your mind racing, trying to keep track of all of the tasks that need to be accomplished in the day, and your feet hit the floor running. When you are in this mode, by the time bedtime arrives you have not even taken a moment to catch your breath, you flop into bed with your mind racing in order to keep track of tomorrow's "To-Do List," and your body is physically exhausted. The problem is that you do not get a restful sleep, your body does not get the opportunity to restore itself from the stresses of the day, and you begin the next day not re-energized and renewed, but depleted, exhausted and frustrated. Your tank is empty and you have nothing left to give, yet the demands of your schedule keep you stuck in this cycle. The fact is that your body cannot sustain this insanity indefinitely. Your body can adapt to any environment you provide, whether it be positive or negative, but it can only do that for a finite period of time before the organs and systems begin to break down under the stresses and the constant demands you place upon them. This is then when disease processes begin to ensue, and signs and symptoms begin to show up. I am here to tell you that this is reversible. How? Because it is YOU who is in charge of your schedule. This is also not easy at times, but I am here to say that without your health, what is the point? I encourage you to make a shift not only in priorities but also in regards to the idea of judgement.

It took many years to be able to release judgement, and when this happened then also came acceptance and the understanding that I am enough! This also brought freedom.

When you are able to release the heavy burdens of living your life always trying to please others, you actually have the opportunity to breathe, live out your desires, and make the shift to living a life that you truly love. I feel this to be one of the greatest shifts I made during my journey to incorporating self-love into my life.

When you are always doing for others, serving others and relying on the views of others to feed into your self-worth, you are not living your reality. Instead, you are living their reality. Remember how I mentioned earlier that no two people perceive the same event in the same way because each of their life experiences are completely different? With this understanding, I was able to release so much stress from my life. When I made the shift to perceive my self-worth from within, this released me from having to rely on the false realities that others would project upon me. I no longer had to claim what was their perceived truth.

When you live your life from your true heart centre, always striving to do your best, and releasing all of the baggage you take on from others, everything changes. Stress levels decrease, happiness increases, relationships improve, there is a dramatic shift in your energy, and life becomes so much more fun to live.

This does not mean that you need to stop doing for others; it simply means that when you begin to incorporate "Me Time" in your daily routine you will be able to give from a cup which is full, rather than running on empty and feeling exhausted and miserable all of the time. The result will be that you will actually be able to give so much more to others because now you will have more energy, you will be well rested, your emotions will be in check, your body will be strong, and your relationships will be well nourished.

I encourage you to release the image of trying to be everything to everyone, and let go of the trappings of trying to be superhuman, for this is never realistically achievable.

6-Where Do You Want Your Journey To Take You?

It is now that I would like you to take a step back and take a look at how you schedule your time and your resources throughout your day. Now is when you can begin to identify if there is balance for you, or if a shift in priorities is in order. Observation is the first step. From there, you can determine what changes you would like to make in order to obtain a greater sense of balance in your life. My recommendation is that the next step be for you to determine what kind of activities you would like to add to your day in order for you to begin taking care of YOU and practicing self-love. Sometimes the first thing to come to mind when beginning to add activities to your schedule is that of exercise and physical activity. But this is not necessarily the best place to start. What we are after here are any activities that you have an interest in or a desire to do. Broadening your horizons and learning something new truly does re-energize your mind and nourish your spirit. When was the last time that you tried something new? My grandmother lived to be 93 years old and Baba always said, "So long as you learn something new each day, only then can you take the rest of the day off." I took this advice to heart and I still follow it daily.

Do you remember when you succeeded at a task for the first time? Do you recall the sense of accomplishment you felt, and the exhilaration of successfully completing something that you worked so hard at? Do you remember when you learned to ride a bike, and the first time that you did it all on your own without training wheels? There may have been cheering, applause, and celebration of your success. Now that may have been a long time ago, so think back to something more recent that you accomplished, and how that made you feel. When you increase your experiences and travel through emotion, this is when life is truly being lived with enthusiasm and vitality.

There are so many different life experiences that each of us has access to. You just have to choose where you want to start.

It is funny, the things that we are taught to believe about ourselves. Growing up I came to believe that I was not artistic at all. It came to the point where I would always tell others I could not draw a stick figure to save my life, and that I didn't have an artistic bone in my body. I labeled myself and would say "I am a doctor," "I am a scientist," "I am not an artist and I am not creative." These limiting self-beliefs put me in a box, and trapped my true abilities and my potential. When you take the step to challenge your own beliefs, and the limits you place upon yourself, growth occurs. As an example I will share with you the time I attended my first paint night. This certainly was nothing serious, and I was not expecting anything of it as I viewed it as supporting a friend at a fundraiser. We did have a lot of fun and by the end of it even my painting was recognizable as a barn.

When I went home that night my family was asleep and I left my painting on the kitchen table. I had projected my limiting self-beliefs of myself onto my family as well, for they too believed that I could not paint. The reason I know this is from the comments that were made in the morning. Jake is always the first one down to get ready for school, and when he arrived in the kitchen for breakfast and saw the painting on the table he said, "Hey, that is a neat painting, but why are you spending money on a piece of art when our walls are already full?" When I told him that I did not purchase a piece of art but that it was something that I created he exclaimed, "YOU painted THAT??" To which I proudly replied "Yes I did!" We all had a good laugh.

I'll also share with you that when I first started working with my business mentor, he suggested that I write a book. Again I declared "I am a doctor," "I am a scientist," "I am not a writer and I am not an author." Once again that limiting self-belief is an untruth, as right now you are reading a book that I am very proud to say I have authored!

I would like you to open up your imagination and think back to some of the dreams and desires you may have had that you did not act upon. Bring those to the present moment. Recognize some of the self-talk and limiting beliefs that show up in your day. I encourage you to try new things, fulfill your desires, and shatter those limits. It is not always easy to successfully accomplish new tasks but that is the whole point. Putting in time and effort, learning new skills and expanding your talents is creative energy, and as we know all energy shifts our perception of our own reality. Think now about some activities that interest and excite you, and sign up for a class or a course, or just start doing it on your own. You will see how this feeds into your heart and soul, re-energizes your batteries and fills your cup so that you can then share more of you with those around you, and start creating a life that you love.

It is my hope now that you can see that in the long run, practicing self-love is not selfish at all.

In the next chapter I will be sharing with you what it is that your engine truly needs in order to run effectively and efficiently. Are you ready to dive in?

When, If Not Now?

Record Your W.I.N.N.s Here

_____

_____

_____

_____

_____

_____

_____

_____

_____

_____

_____

_____

_____

_____

_____

_____

_____

_____

_____

_____

_____

_____

_____

_____

_____

_____

_____

Chapter 3

What Your Body Needs

The doctor of the future will no longer treat the human frame with drugs, but rather will cure and prevent disease with nutrition.
—Thomas Edison

1-Air

In the previous chapter I discussed how you can begin to incorporate self-love in the outside realm of your being. Now I would like to dive into what your body requires on the inside in order for optimal health to be expressed.

I find that the majority of people, who seek me out to help them improve their health and overall well-being, really do not know how their body functions on the inside. If you find yourself wondering the same thing, I am here to tell you that it is not your fault! This information is not taught in school or in life. The government, lobbyists, corporations, and the media all have such a strong presence, along with a specific agenda, in your day-to-day life that it is very difficult not to be confused after being overloaded with misinformation. Remember that for the majority of the time the sole purpose of the media is to sell you something, and not necessarily share the truth with you. Throughout this chapter I will share with you the physiology and science behind what your body needs in order to function optimally.

I have experienced through working with my clients that often when they are eating something — let's take for example the fast food burger — not much thought is given as to what happens from when it goes in one end and comes out the other. I am here to change all of that for you. The miraculous creation of the human body and all of the bodily processes which continue to function even without you consciously being aware of it, is often taken for granted. The brain is the master controller, and continuously regulates every single system, organ and cell without you even realizing or understanding the intricacies of what is involved to keep you not just alive, but healthy, happy and vibrant.

In this chapter it is my intention to help shed some light on the miraculous functions which happen within your body during the entire course of your existence. I have found that when working with my clients, when I share this understanding it changes everything, which then accelerates the pace at which they reach their goals. The reason for this is that when they are able to make educated choices while having their goals in mind, they have a clear roadmap to their destination. They are no longer taking the scenic route with many detours.

Let's begin with the most critical need of the body. Without this there is zero function of any of the mechanisms, pathways and processes, and life ceases to exist. I can only survive minutes without this critical substance. Are you able to guess what I am referring to?

The most vital substance required by the body is AIR! I can only survive minutes without breathing. Without my breath, every single system within my body will cease to function, and death will be the result.

You may not often think of this because it is so automatic, and your brain regulates it so perfectly that you are not even conscious of it. When you begin to consider your breath you realize that when you are sitting at rest your breath is at rest. When you begin to exercise or do something strenuous the rate of your breathing also increases. This is because oxygen is necessary in order for your body to create energy for your muscles, cells, and tissues. Your body is then able to physiologically perform the exercise or activity. The brain is the greatest consumer of

34

energy in your body. It processes all of the information that comes in through your senses of sight, smell, touch, taste and hearing. Your brain is constantly busy whether you are awake or asleep. It constantly requires energy in order to function. When the body does not receive enough oxygen, the brain is the first organ to be damaged. Without a functioning brain there is no function of the physical body. This is how vital air is for your survival.

Breathing does not require any conscious thought. Your breathing also fluctuates to accommodate whatever situation you may be in. Your breathing changes during the sleep cycles, when you are sitting quietly, when you are stressed, when you are sad, when you are exercising, when you are relaxed, and it is even affected by your thoughts. Your breath is forever adapting to your current situation, and it is completely regulated by the brain.

It is a common perception that air comes in through the nose or mouth, goes into the lungs, and then back out through the nose or mouth. In actual fact air does come in through the nose and mouth, but once it reaches the lungs the oxygen dissolves into the bloodstream. (It may be helpful to think of the blood stream as being the delivery system or the highway within your body.) The blood stream then delivers the oxygen to every single cell within your body, even as far away as your baby toe, because energy production happens at the cellular level and it requires oxygen.

With this understanding it becomes evident that if you improve your breathing technique you will also increase the efficiency of energy production within your body. This will lead to enhanced vitality and optimal health. Be sure to go to http://DrStaceyCooper.com and enter your name and email address to receive the free video series "Eliminate Your 5 Hidden Energy Drainers™." Here is where I demonstrate healthy breathing techniques for you to incorporate right now into your daily routine.

Let's now examine your breathing style. As you are sitting right now notice how you breathe. I would like you to understand that your lungs occupy the majority of the space within your rib cage. Your lungs are large in order to deliver large amounts of oxygen to your entire body;

however, your breathing often does not reflect this. Does your body move very much while you breathe as you are sitting motionless, reading this book? Generally speaking, most people will notice that perhaps only their shoulders will move only slightly while they are breathing quietly. This is an energy drainer and is very inefficient breathing for your body. Now go to the free video series and I will teach you how to create effective breathing patterns.

When you begin to become more conscious about your breathing style and incorporate techniques to improve the delivery of oxygen throughout your body, your energy levels will increase and you will also experience decreased physical stress of your systems, a calming of your being, and improved health.

2-Water

Now let's think of the second most critical component that your body requires for survival. You may be surprised to learn what it is. Did you know that your body can survive for extended periods of time without food? Due to the energy reserves found in the form of adipose tissue, the fat stores in your body, this enables you to survive for a period of time without food. In the event that all of the fat stores are depleted your body can also break down muscle tissue for energy production. This is not ideal but it is another form of available energy. This enables you to be able to survive for months without any food. Due to this fact, food is not the second most critical component for the survival of your body. Can you now guess what the second most critical component for optimal health of your body is?

The second most critical component is water. Your body is only able to survive for three days without water. This occurs because, when you are not consuming enough water, your body tissues will start to draw water out of the blood. As this occurs the transportation of oxygen throughout your body slows down and sometimes stops, which leads to the shutting down of the organs in the body. The human body can start to shut down and begin to die with as little as nine to twelve percent water loss. Now I would like you to reflect for a moment and think about how much water you consume in a day. Or do you not drink water at all? To illustrate how important proper hydration is for your body, it has been scientifically concluded that the average human body contains approximately 37.2 trillion cells and there is not one cell that can survive without water. Your body is made up of 70 to 75% water, and every single cellular process requires water. Your brain content is 83% water, your blood and eyes are 95% water, your kidneys and lungs 83% water, and your muscles including your heart muscle are 75% water.

When it comes to hydrating your body not all fluids are created equal. Some are absorbed more readily than others, while some fluids actually remove water from your system. These are called diuretics. Examples of these water-depleting substances are caffeinated beverages. The right sources of hydration for your body are important in keeping energy production at optimal levels.

The best source of hydration is water. A point to remember here is that there are many sources of water, and they are not all created equal. I will be discussing sources of water in greater depth in Chapter 5. For hydrating your body, water is all you need. It is simple, does not require complicated processing, and it is absorbed readily. In order to reach optimal hydration levels the amount of water you consume is related to your body size, weight and activity level, and also where you live. As a general guideline, each day you should try to drink between half an ounce and an ounce of water for each pound you weigh. For example, if you weigh 150 pounds, that would be 75 to 150 ounces of water a day. This may seem like a lot at first, but your system will quickly balance out to your new water load. From a scientific standpoint there is an easy way to determine the hydration level of your body. You can do this in the privacy of your own home and at no cost to you. This is the "P" test. When your body is well hydrated your urine will be clear, colourless, and odourless. When you are in a state of dehydration the last place your body can absorb water from is your elimination organs— your bowel and bladder. The more dehydrated your body is the more concentrated your urine becomes and your stool becomes more firm. Your urine will also appear more cloudy, darker in colour and have a greater odour. As a side note, urine is acidic, and the more concentrated it becomes the more corrosive it is to the bladder wall. For good bladder health it is important to keep well hydrated with the right sources of water and to be sure to pass the "P" test. Your bowel function will also be improved when you are well hydrated. With dehydration comes constipation, and with constipation comes many other issues, so be sure to improve your bowel health by increasing your water intake.

The wrong sources of hydration include all liquids that contain anything more than just water. Commercial fruit juices are full of sugar and do not contain any fibre or other healthful nutrients. Many of them are produced by soft drink manufacturers. So-called "electrolyte" drinks contain colours, chemicals, and preservatives, and are not as healthy as you are led to believe through advertising and the media. Soft drinks and soda pop are of no nutritional value whatsoever, and there is not one good thing I have to say about them. They are full of chemicals, carcinogens, colouring and sweeteners, which are of no benefit to your system. They are also so acidic that just one glass of pop or soda dramatically alters the pH of your body which then must be buffered to maintain balance within your system. (pH of the body will be discussed in Chapter 5.) Aspartame is very commonly found in pop, and is linked to brain cancer and Alzheimer's disease. Phosphoric acid weakens bones and rots your teeth. Artificial sweeteners actually make you crave more calories, which seems to go completely against the reason why you would be consuming that product in the first place. Artificial colouring is purely cosmetic, and is tainted with carcinogens. High fructose corn syrup increases body fat, cholesterol, and triglyceride levels, and it also makes you hungry. Potassium benzoate is a preservative and is metabolized by your body into benzene, which is a carcinogen. Food dyes in pops and sodas lead to impaired brain function, hyperactive behaviour and lack of impulse control. All of these ingredients are commonly found in sodas and pops. Do you think any of these things are good for improving your body function? I don't!

Now let's explore some other options for hydrating your body. There are other fluids which are commonly consumed and actually take water out of your body. Beverages containing caffeine fall into this category, and are classed as diuretics. Coffee, tea, and soda pops are all examples of diuretics, and lead to dehydration of the body. Does your day not begin until you have had your morning coffee? If this is the case then I ask you to check in with yourself and see how you feel at 10am. When you hit the mid-morning slump this is the crash and burn cycle. Caffeine is not an energy booster; it is an energy drainer. You can see exactly why this is the case in my free video series "Eliminate your Hidden Energy Drainers™" at http://DrStaceyCooper.com. Stimulation from an outside source is not necessary for your body. If you are providing good fuels for your body, then your body will be able to create all of the energy that your system requires. A common thought is that caffeine is a quick energy booster. This form of energy is extremely short-lived as it is metabolized very quickly, and it places great stress on your adrenal system and cortisol levels. (Cortisol is the stress hormone in your body.) Consuming caffeine leads to a rise in cortisol levels in your body. This revs up your system, and it stays revved up for as long as the stimulus is present. Caffeine, however, does not last long as it is metabolized very quickly, and when it is broken down this is when the crash occurs. Have you ever experienced the jitters when you have consumed too much coffee? This is the adrenal system being revved up and running out of control. This will also affect your blood pressure and heart rate levels in a negative way. When this type of stimulus is provided on a regular basis the system is not given the chance to come back to a resting idle. When the engine is continuously revved up, the parts start to wear out. There are much better sources of fuel for your body, which prevent this crash and burn cycle from occurring.

Becoming more conscious of your choices for hydrating your body will lead to an improvement in your body function, resulting in enhanced energy production at the cellular level. This will progress to improved metabolism and lead to weight loss and enhanced vitality naturally.

3-Protein

Did you know that, next to water, protein is the most plentiful substance in your body?

Protein is a nutrient that the body needs to grow and maintain itself. According to US and Canadian guidelines, women need to consume 46 g of protein per day while men need to consume 56 g of protein per day to avoid a deficiency.

Now I will share with you something that may surprise you. Every single cell in your body has some form of protein in it. In addition there are other important parts of your body such as your hair, skin, eyes and body organs which are all made from proteins. Many substances that control body functions, such as enzymes and hormones, are also made from protein. Other important functions of protein in your body include forming blood cells and making antibodies to protect you from illness and infections. From all of this you can see that protein is vital for every function of your body, and this is why what you have heard is true, that protein is essential at every meal.

Protein is made up of many particles. The building blocks which are used to make up protein molecules are called amino acids. There are different kinds of amino acids available for your body, and they fall into two categories. There are non-essential amino acids as well as essential amino acids. The essential amino acids are labeled this way because it is *essential* that you obtain them through your diet. Non-essential amino acids can be created within your body from all of the other building blocks that you supply to your body.

Now let's explore where most of your protein comes from. What is the first thing that comes to your mind when you think of sources of protein? When you think about food sources the common answer for a protein source is meat. Muscles of the body are made up of protein, and it is these muscles from animals that we eat as a source of animal protein.

All of the essential amino acids can be found in each meat source of protein. This means that meat is a complete protein because it contains the full complement of the essential amino acids, but this does not mean that it is good for you.

Plant protein sources are labelled incomplete proteins because they do not contain the full complement of all of the essential amino acids in one plant. Plant sources of protein include legumes, grains, nuts, seeds and fruits.

On a worldwide basis plant protein foods contribute over 60% of the per capita supply of protein on average. In North America, animal derived foods contribute about 70% of the protein sources. For the whole rest of the world 60% of their protein comes strictly from plants. When you look at the incidence of obesity in North America, do you think there is something wrong?

For sources of plant proteins, legumes are one of the best sources, with quinoa being the only complete protein from a plant source. Legumes are a more complete protein than whole grains and cereals. Whole grains and cereals are incomplete proteins, as they tend to be limited in the amino acid lysine or threonine, both of which are available in other plant sources. This is why it is important to combine plant sources of proteins so that you get the full complement of all of the amino acids every day.

Strict vegans (those who do not eat any animal products including eggs or dairy) are able to get enough essential amino acids by eating a variety of plant proteins and by combining them. If you do not eat animal products, it is important to eat different types of plant foods together or within the same day to get the proper balance and amount of essential amino acids that your body requires. Combining beans and rice, or lentils and barley, or nut butter and steel cut wheat free oats will provide all of the essential amino acids in the right amounts. These food combinations mix foods from different plant groups to complement the amino acids provided by each. Combining foods from any two of the following plant groups will provide you with a higher quality protein.

For your convenience I have provided a list for easy reference.

- Legumes - beans, peas, lentils, soybeans, kidney beans, white beans, mung beans, chickpeas, cowpeas, lima beans, pigeon peas, and lupines
- Nuts - almonds, brazil nuts, cashews, walnuts, hazelnuts, pecans, and pistachios
- Seeds - cotton, pumpkin, sesame, sunflower, chia, sesame, flax, and hemp hearts
- Fruits - dried apricots, raisins, guava, dates, prunes, avocado, kumquat, jackfruit, currants, raspberries, bananas, peaches, figs, grapefruit, and cantaloupe
- Grains - buckwheat, steel-cut oats, millet, rice, sorghum, amaranth, and quinoa

Providing your body with a variety of complex fuels from a variety of sources can result in balanced nutrition, optimal functioning of your body, and enhanced vitality.

4-Fats

Discussing fats can seem scary because they have been given such a bad rap. So much information in the media states consuming a low fat diet is a healthy way of living, and that fats are to be avoided at all cost. You may also be confused about which fats are the bad fats, and which ones are the good fats. I am here to help you sort through the confusion and give you a clear view of what your body requires on a physiological level.

It is a misconception that a low-fat intake equals healthier living. This could not be further from the truth! When fat is removed from a food product, sugar must be added in order to make it taste good again. Therefore, consuming low-fat products actually increases your sugar intake and leads to the diabetic connection, and it is now the sugar that is making you fat. In regards to fat requirements for your body and how your body functions, when you starve your body of fat this actually leads to a breakdown in neurological function and results in the progression of degenerative diseases throughout many systems in your body.

Therefore consuming a low-fat diet is not healthy at all.

Providing healthy fats for your body is critical because every single cell membrane throughout the entire body is made up of fat. By not providing the essential nutrients for your body, the result is decreased energy production along with deterioration and degeneration of tissues, organs and systems. Your brain is composed of 83% water, as mentioned earlier, and it is the organ in the body with the greatest fat content, consisting of a minimum of 60% fat. Even though the brain represents only 2% of the total body weight of an average adult, it consumes 20% of the energy produced by the body.

Science has shown that fatty acids are among the most crucial molecules that determine your brain's integrity and ability to perform. An imbalance in dietary intake of fatty acids is associated with impaired brain performance and neurological disease. When your fat intake is restricted, the first organ to begin to 'starve' and deteriorate is your brain. The result is a decrease in neurological function which leads to degenerative diseases of the nervous system such as Multiple Sclerosis and brain dysfunction such as dementia and Alzheimers disease.

Did you know that at the earliest moment of development, after the sperm and egg unite and the cells multiply, the brain and spinal cord are the very first system to be developed? The brain is the master control centre of every single cellular function within your entire body. Without a functioning brain the body cannot survive. This is evident when someone has sustained a serious injury and the brain has been severely damaged. In this state the physical body cannot survive without artificial measures being taken. The physical body must then be placed on life support systems in order to maintain functions within the body and keep the tissues alive. Providing healthy fats for your body is critical because every single cell membrane throughout your entire body is made up of fat. Not providing essential nutrients that your body requires will result in decreased function, reduced metabolism and decreased energy production. Without consuming healthy fats your cell walls become weak and leaky. If the cell wall is not intact then the transporters which deliver components into the cell cannot do their job. Leaky cell membranes mean that the cellular components will not stay inside the cell where they are supposed to be. Cellular metabolism will cease to occur because the cell is no longer a well functioning unit due to the disruption of its membrane. This leads to ineffective cellular metabolism.

Good fats in your diet are essential for transporting all of the fat-soluble vitamins into your cells. The fat-soluble vitamins are vitamins A, D, E, K and beta-carotene. Each of these vitamins performs specific vital functions within your body. Without good fats present in your diet, you would suffer from nutrient deficiencies as the fat-soluble vitamins would not be able to get into the cells. Instead, they would just continue to float around in the bloodstream, not being utilized by your body, and then would just be excreted. It has been shown that healthy fats also provide protection against diseases including cancer and heart disease. Now is this not exactly the opposite of what you have heard through the media and advertising? For heart health you are told to use margarine and to avoid fats, and this is just one example. No wonder there is such mass confusion about healthy eating!

There are different categories of fats, and now I will discuss the group called *essential fatty acids*. These fats are essential because it is essential that you receive them from your diet. Your body is not capable of manufacturing them. Your body is an incredible mechanism which can manufacture many different things from what you provide through the foods you eat, but there are some elements that your body just cannot make. These substances are called essential, and the omega-3 and omega-6 essential fatty acids fall into this category. It is necessary that you consume these particular fatty acids from your diet in order to have optimal cellular function and enhanced vitality.

As you can see, healthy fats play a very important role in optimizing many functions of your body. I encourage you to read on as I will discuss easy-to-find sources of healthy fats for your body, and easy ways to implement them into your daily life.

5-Carbohydrates

The role of carbohydrates in the body includes providing energy for working muscles, providing fuel for the central nervous system, enabling metabolization of fat, and preventing protein from being used as energy. What this means is that if you are not providing good fuels for your body and you do not have enough carbohydrates in your system, your body will go into starvation mode. It will then utilize whatever it can to create energy, and its next default source of energy is protein, which it will get by metabolizing your own muscle tissue. This will lead to muscle wasting. As you can imagine, losing muscle is not of benefit to your body! Here is another way that muscle tissue can be affected by metabolization within the body. You may already know that cancer occurs in the body when some cells begin to reproduce and metabolize at a faster rate than normal. The control mechanisms for normal cellular function have become faulty, and cellular reproduction then spirals out of control. Cancer is a group of normal cells that have gone awry, and are working faster than the rest of the body. It generally starts in a localized area, and it requires a lot of energy for a tumour to grow. This is what leads to muscle wasting. Because the tumour has such a huge energy requirement to sustain itself, it will consume every source of energy that is available to it. This includes using the protein from muscle tissue as a source of energy. This is why there is evidence of rapid weight loss and muscle wasting in cancer patients.

Carbohydrates are the preferred source of fuel for muscle contraction and cellular metabolism, because they are a simple fuel that is easy for your body to break down and use. When you eat carbs, your body metabolizes them and breaks them down into simple sugars called glucose. The glucose molecules are then absorbed into the bloodstream. As the sugar level rises in your blood, the pancreas releases a hormone called insulin. Insulin is a carrier in your body which is needed to move sugar from the blood into the cells, where it can be used as a source of energy. When metabolization occurs quickly — as with simple sugars (simple fuels are already broken down to the simplest building blocks through processing) — you are more likely to feel hungry again soon. When metabolization occurs more slowly, as with complex fuels (complex fuels are whole foods which have not been processed and have all of their components intact), you will be satisfied longer. Complex carbohydrates give you energy over a longer period of time. The carbohydrates in some foods (mostly those that contain a lot of simple sugars) cause the blood sugar level to rise more quickly than others, and this leads to health problems like diabetes and heart disease.

Carbohydrates are classed as either simple or complex. Simple carbohydrates are also called simple sugars, and are found in refined products like white sugar and flour. You will also find simple sugars in more nutritious foods, such as fruits and vegetables. It is better to get your simple sugars from whole food sources because they are a source of natural unrefined sugar and they also contain vitamins, nutrients, and most importantly fibre. It is the fibre in whole foods which helps to slow down the metabolization process, and allow a much more gradual release of sugar into your bloodstream.

A lollipop, for example, has lots of added refined sugar and does not contain any nutrients or fibre. This leads to the consumption of needless calories with no nutritional benefit, and also to the spiking of blood sugar levels.

Complex carbohydrates are also called starches. Starches include grain products, such as bread, crackers, pasta, and rice. As with simple sugars, some complex carbohydrate foods are better choices than others. Refined grains, such as white flour and white rice, have been processed, and this removes much of the nutrients and the fibre, while unrefined grains still have their vitamin and mineral content intact. Unrefined grains are also rich in fibre, which helps your digestive system work well. Fibre helps you to feel full, and this makes you less likely to overeat these foods. This factor explains why a bowl of steel cut oatmeal fills you up better than sugary candy, even though both items have the same amount of calories.

As you can see, if you are not meeting the nutritional requirements of your body, and you are fuelling it with bad fuels, it will function to the best of its ability, but it will not function optimally.

You can provide 'high test' fuel for your engine by implementing the easy and delicious recipes from my Healthy Fuels Cookbook™. It won't take long for you to see how performance of your body is enhanced with the burning of clean healthy fuels. All four of our children can make all of the recipes, and they love eating them too.

For a copy of my Healthy Fuels Cookbook™ simply visit http://DrStaceyCooper.com. You can purchase the cookbook as a PDF, or for a personally autographed copy of the coil bound book simply email me at drstacey@drstaceycooper.com with subject line: cookbook.

You may have found some of the information in this chapter to be surprising, and it may even challenge what you thought to be true. I have found that when my clients and patients come to understand how the body functions physiologically, it is so much easier to get on the right track to optimal health. It has nothing to do with diets.

In the next chapter perhaps you may take a big sigh of relief as I explain the mechanism behind why diets don't work. Read on to see why it is not your fault if you feel like you were not successful at dieting. In truth your body was really successful at adapting to the environment that you provided for it. Diets are designed to fail, and I can tell you that it has nothing to do with a lack of willpower.

When, If Not Now?

Record Your W.I.N.N.s Here

_____

_____

_____

_____

_____

_____

_____

_____

_____

_____

_____

_____

_____

_____

_____

_____

_____

_____

_____

_____

_____

_____

_____

Chapter 4

Why Diets Don't Work

A mind that is stretched by a new experience can never go back to its old dimensions.
—Oliver Wendell Holmes Jr.

1-Your Brain Is In Control, Not Your Stomach

Did you know that your brain, and not your stomach, is in control of letting you know when you are thirsty, hungry, or when you are craving? When working one-on-one with my clients I often discover that not much thought is given as to what the body does with what is provided for it. Let's take, for example, a fast food burger. It just goes in one end and comes out the other end without any thought given as to what happens in between. In actual fact we do not have to consciously think about the process at all. It all happens automatically.

Did you know that your entire digestive system is simply one long tube? Food does go in one end and come out the other, but all of the nutrients have to be absorbed into the body along the way. (See illustration on the next page.)

The remarkable design is such that no process in the body acts on its own. Every single function is under the close control of many systems within your body. Now I shall give you a brief generalized rundown as to the systems that are involved during the transition from the food on your plate to the delivery of nutrients to the cells in your body.

Digestive System

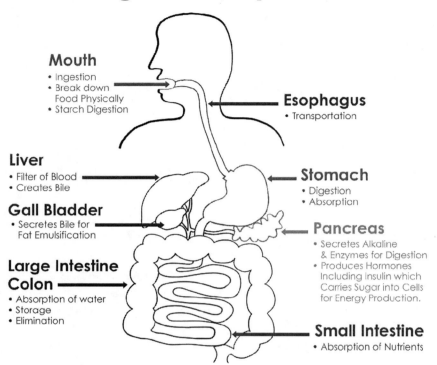

Mouth
• Ingestion
• Break down
  Food Physically
• Starch Digestion

Esophagus
• Transportation

Liver
• Filter of Blood
• Creates Bile

Stomach
• Digestion
• Absorption

Gall Bladder
• Secretes Bile for
  Fat Emulsification

Pancreas
• Secretes Alkaline
  & Enzymes for Digestion
• Produces Hormones
  Including Insulin which
  Carries Sugar into Cells
  for Energy Production.

**Large Intestine
Colon**
• Absorption of water
• Storage
• Elimination

Small Intestine
• Absorption of Nutrients

Your brain and nervous system are the computer of your body, and regulate every single cell and all of their functions. Your brain is the master controller. Did you know that this system is so vital that it is the very first system to develop after fertilization of the egg? Without the brain and spinal cord there is no life.

Your endocrine system regulates hormone balances and enzyme secretions. Enzymes are extremely important during your digestive process because they help to break down the foods that you eat into the tiny molecular building blocks that your cells need to utilize in order to carry out all of their functions.

The satiation centre in your brain triggers the feelings of hunger and thirst. (The mechanism of the satiation centre will be discussed in detail later in this chapter.) The satiation centre is extremely important and it is not being used well at all. The North American food manufacturing process has been a key factor in sabotaging this natural mechanism in your brain which controls your food intake. Highly processed foods have resulted in lower volume and higher caloric density consumption, which leads directly to obesity. As you can see, the industrialized food manufacturing process is leading you away from health and directly towards disease. This is not progress.

Your gastric system is where digestion of the food you eat occurs. Your stomach is basically a holding tank where your food can be worked on by the digestive enzymes that your body produces. The enzymes break down the large food particles into the smallest building blocks which can then be absorbed into your bloodstream and distributed throughout the rest of your body where they can be utilized.

Your intestinal system is where your body absorbs all of the nutrients that you have provided for it. If your intestines cannot absorb the nutrients from the foodstuffs you have provided, then in essence there is no fuel for the engine available as all of it will be voided out of your body.

Your circulatory system is vital in delivering the nutrients, which are the source of energy, to every single cell within your body, even those as far away as your baby toe. This system is also responsible for transporting all of the waste products from each cell, after they have produced energy, to your elimination organs — your bowel and bladder, your skin and your lungs.

As you can see now, there is plenty involved every single time you put something into your mouth, and the consumption of food is not just 'in one end and out the other.' You do not have to consciously think about the process, but there are many systems, enzymes, processes and cells involved, and it is all done automatically. The human body is a miraculous machine, and it pays to fuel your engine well in order to experience optimal body function, enhanced vitality, and improved quality of life.

2-Your Reward Cascade

Did you know that there are many different mechanisms that function in your brain which hinder your weight loss efforts? The reward cascade is one of these mechanisms, and it is one of the major underlying factors as to why diets and dieting are not successful for long-lasting weight loss results. This is why modifying your lifestyle choices is the true path to obtaining your health and wellness goals.

When you feel frustrated with dieting and feel like you are failing with your weight loss journey, I am here to tell you it is not your fault. I will share with you how you can have success.

The reward cascade is just one of the mechanisms which is hard-wired in your brain, and it works against you when you are dieting. The reward cascade is also just one of the mechanisms responsible for cravings.

The human brain has not evolved much over the past 10,000 years. During the time when we were hunters and gatherers this reward cascade played a very important role and was critical for our survival. The reward cascade is dopamine-based and is designed to respond to food and other experiences that improve our chances of survival and reproduction. Did you know that all animals have this reward-based system? The reason why our system seems to have gone haywire is because these systems are tuned to the natural environment. Today's industrialized food manufacturing processes have created an artificial environment, and the reward cascade does not differentiate between the two. You are now exposed to 'food stuffs' which are designed to trigger this reward cascade and lead you to have cravings, to spend more money, purchase more products and consume more calories. You feed your cravings and the food manufacturers get rich. This can lead to overstimulation of the reward cascade, and to maladaptive behaviour.

The reward cascade is designed in such a way that we would adapt our behaviours to receive the greatest reward for our efforts in order to ensure our survival. This was an invaluable mechanism when we were hunters and gatherers, as we would seek out food with the highest nutrient and caloric content in order to sustain our survival. The reward cascade ensured that we would not trek for days in search of iceberg lettuce, as this is a very low caloric and low nutrient food source, but we would search for ripe, nutrient dense, caloric rich berries, plants and wild meat. This reward cascade is still hard at work in your brain, even though it is no longer needed for your survival as a hunter and gatherer. With the conveniences available to you today, it is very easy to find very calorie dense foods. The trouble is that these foods are not nutritious, and the calorie to volume ratio is very much out of balance. For example, when you look at a typical chocolate bar, the volume of 'food' is quite small in comparison to the amount of calories contained in the chocolate bar. The result is that your calorie consumption does not match what your brain perceives in regards to the amount of food you have consumed. This leaves you feeling hungry because the stretch receptors in your stomach have not yet been activated and therefore your brain has not received the message from your stomach that it is full. This leads you to reach for more food because your satiation centre has not been activated. (I will discuss the satiation centre in the next section.)

The food qualities which stimulate the reward cascade are sweetness, saltiness and softness. Just think of some of the foods which you may crave. Do you crave sweets, chocolate, or salty foods? The taste buds in your mouth also coincide with these food qualities as your taste buds can detect sweet, sour, bitter, salty and savoury, and food manufacturers have taken great measures to ensure that these food and taste qualities are present in significant amounts in order to trigger your reward cascade as often as possible.

Did you know that recreational drugs like cocaine also act directly on the dopamine reward system? This is why recreational drug use often results in a self-destructive spiral of pleasure-seeking behaviour. Manufactured food is now also leading to the same self-destructive behaviour. Due to the overstimulation of your reward cascade, this mechanism has turned manufactured food into an addiction.

When you begin to fuel your body differently and break out of the reward cascade, you are able to eliminate the crave and begin to experience better body function naturally. I will share with you how to do this in the upcoming chapters.

3-Your Satiation Centre

Today's hectic society has led to the natural hunger response within the body to be altered in such a way that it has become almost non-functioning. This happens when you eat when the clock on the wall tells you to, instead of listening to the natural rhythms of your body and only eating when you are hungry. Take a moment right now and think about how often you eat when you aren't truly hungry. You ate just because the hours on the clock said it was lunchtime. This is not a good thing because you are not following the natural rhythms of your body. This leads to altered hunger patterns; you eat when you are not hungry, and this leads to altered metabolism. This is not progress but in actual fact leads to obesity.

There is a centre in your brain called the satiation centre which alerts you when your energy levels are depleted, and when you should be consuming more food. This is one of the first signals of hunger. With this comes increased production of saliva in your mouth and increased motility in your stomach in anticipation of eating. Your body is getting ready for the food that you are going to give it. You cannot eat if you have a really dry mouth. There are enzymes in your saliva which initiate the digestive process, and this all begins in your mouth. Your stomach is a muscle, and it helps to physically break down the food. In anticipation of food arriving, your stomach will begin to churn. This is when your stomach rumbles or growls. As food is being prepared, all of your senses are involved. You see it, you work with it, you smell it, and your touch receptors are engaged. All of these things lead to a heightened awareness that food is on its way. There will actually be the release of some digestive enzymes into the mouth to start digesting food as soon as your teeth have broken it down physically.

Yes it is true what your mother said, that your stomach does not have teeth, so you better chew your food. Chewing your food well is important for increasing the surface area of the food particles in order for the digestive enzymes to have greater opportunity to break down what you are providing for your system. Chewing your food well will also give your stomach time to get the signals to your brain as to when your stomach is full. When you 'inhale' your food without much chewing, you have the opportunity to ingest many more calories than what would have satisfied your stomach. This is something that leads to weight gain. If you find that you tend to eat too quickly, a great practice is to set your utensils down between each and every mouthful. This will slow down your eating process, you will actually enjoy your food much more, your brain will have the opportunity to catch up to all that you have ingested, and your brain will receive the message from your stomach that you are full with less calorie consumption.

Did you know that there are receptors in your stomach which gauge how much you eat? This is really quite a remarkable system. There are two different kinds of receptors in your stomach which relay information to the satiation centre in your brain. There are stretch receptors which gauge how much food is in your stomach. The stomach is made up of muscle, as is your entire digestive system. As more food enters your stomach it begins to stretch like a balloon does when you fill it with water. As the stomach stretches more, the stretch receptors send signals to the satiation centre in your brain to let you know that you are getting full. The second set of receptors are density receptors. These receptors determine the caloric density or the richness of the food you are ingesting. For instance, 500 calories of natural plant food fills your stomach completely, and this will trigger both the stretch receptors and the caloric density receptors to stimulate the satiation centre in your brain to alert you that you have had enough to eat. This is when you then put down your utensils and back away from the table. However, when you consume 500 calories of processed caloric rich food, such as a chocolate bar, this is a low-volume and high-caloric density food and it only partially fills your stomach. This deceives your satiation centre, which in turn tells your brain you need to eat more. Now your satiation centre is being deceived, which leads to miscommunication throughout the system, and you end up consuming needless calories.

High fructose corn syrup and processed sugars are much more

calorie dense than the plants they are made from. The dramatic increase in their use in food production is just one of the major reasons why our diets have become more calorie dense, the satiation centre has been tricked, and the incidence of obesity is on the rise.

4-Your Addiction Centre

With today's food manufacturing processes and how easy it is to obtain food stuffs which are very dense in calories, food has become a low grade addiction. When you change how you fuel your body, you can break this food addiction cycle. The key is to understand the motivational triad which controls it all.

The motivational triad is a trio of mechanisms which is present in every creature because it is necessary for survival in order to continue to pass genetic information on from one generation to the next.

The first step in the triad is pleasure seeking. There are only two basic needs that feed into this loop: food and procreation. Without multiplication of the species, it would become extinct. This is survival of the fittest. This is what every species, every animal, every plant, every thing is meant to do on the earth. Without food or procreation your genes would not be passed on.

The second step is pain avoidance. Back when we were hunters and gatherers, you would not go walking into the den of a lion and think that you are going to have him for dinner, because he would certainly be the one who was going to have you for dinner. Pain avoidance is a vital survival mechanism.

The third step is doing everything with the least amount of effort. This is energy conservation.

With this motivational triad being hard-wired into your system, you are programed in such a way that richer foods excite your senses to a greater degree. As hunters and gatherers, you did not want to go looking for iceberg lettuce and get minimal return for your energy investment. You wanted great return for your energy expenditure when you had to travel long distances for your food. You wanted the highest amount of dietary reward with the least amount of effort. This has helped our ancestors find the most calorie dense and ripe foods available which contributed to survival. The issue presents itself in today's environment as food manufacturers artificially increase the caloric density of foods resulting in giving us a hyper amount of pleasure and leading us into this 'pleasure trap.' This is how drug addiction works, and our food has now become a low-grade addiction.

When you ingest highly processed refined foods you enter the pleasure trap. During food manufacturing, fibre from the original raw food has been removed, as has water and minerals. Everything has been done in order to hyper-concentrate the sugar and fat content, and salt has been added as well. If you consume only artificial foods, you must overeat in terms of volume in order to be satisfied. This ties back to the satiation centre which we discussed earlier. This consumption of unnaturally caloric dense foods has become the main cause of the epidemic of obesity in North America. It isn't that you have become more self-indulgent or lazier, it is that the mechanisms of your satiation centre are being fooled.

Wheat, when ingested, gets broken down into molecules which, once they are delivered to the brain, follow the pathway called the "opiate cascade." This is the addiction centre in the brain. Wheat does this because, when it is broken down, its chemical structure is extremely similar to that of opiates, and this is why the wheat molecules then follow this pathway. This is the root of cravings. When you ingest wheat, you feel good due to the triggering of the opiate cascade. This is how wheat-based products become know as "comfort foods." Because wheat is a simple fuel, it is metabolized quickly, and when that fuel has been metabolized and there is no more available to the body, you fall into a withdrawal pattern, which is when the craving begins. The brain is telling the body that it has run out of that "feel good" molecule and now you are franticly searching for more. The thing is, if you were truly hungry you would eat the carrot sticks in the fridge. You are not hungry, you are just craving. Food manufacturers know this about wheat, and that is why they add it to products where you would never imagine wheat to be found. Wheat is present in tomato soup, taco seasoning mix, salad dressings, pumpkin pie filling, and the list goes on and on.

This is to ensure that the feel good cascade gets triggered, which means that you then crave more, which results in you eating more needless calories while the food manufacturing companies get rich!

I am here to tell you that not all is lost. There is a way to avoid this. It is possible to get rid of the majority of your cravings altogether. Yes, wheat does travel through the addiction centre of the brain, but the good news is that it is a much easier addiction to quit than smoking for example. I can tell you that with just 5 days of being wheat and gluten free you will already realize noticeable changes in the functioning of your body. Within 5 days you will experience a decrease in intestinal bloating and abdominal upset, a decrease in heartburn, indigestion and acid reflux. You will also notice the lack of craving which occurs once you eliminate wheat and gluten from your diet. As months progress and you remain committed to excluding wheat and gluten from your lifestyle, you will notice even more remarkable changes as your body begins to repair itself. These changes are the reversal of disease processes. Ill-health conditions and diseases can actually be reversed as the inflammation in the body is eliminated and healing can occur. I have patients who have experienced the reversal of celiac disease, colitis, Crohn's disease, liver disorders and cardiovascular disease.

Remember that when you change the environment that you provide for your body in a positive fashion, it will adapt to the new environment, and this is when reversal of disease processes and healing can occur. To see how easy it is to start to make positive changes for your environment and how to "Kick your Cravings for Good," go to http://GetHealthyQuickStart.com where you can view my free 3-part training series discussing how to kick cravings for good.

5-The Crash and Burn Cycle

As I have mentioned previously, you now know that the purpose of your body is to maintain homeostasis. This means that all of your systems are balanced in their function. Times of stress, either positive stress or negative, take your body away from the balance point of homeostasis. Your body thrives when blood sugar levels are maintained instead of peeking and falling. Cortisol is the stress hormone in your body, and provides a vital function for your survival; however, when cortisol levels are artificially elevated this is when your body is not able to come back to a resting level. As with our analogy of your body being like an engine, when your cortisol levels are high and your engine is revving uncontrollably, your parts begin to wear out.

A commonly held notion is that stimulation of your system is needed from an outside source. This is not true. Something you can think about here is your morning coffee. If you start your day with a coffee how do you feel at 10 AM? As you are coming into a low energy state this is the crash and burn! Caffeine is not an energy booster, it is an energy drainer. I invite you to learn more about your five hidden energy drainers by reviewing my free video series at DrStaceyCooper.com. Simply enter your name and email address in the box and you will immediately receive this free 2 part video series and the accompanying mind map which appears on page 4 in Chapter 1.

Stimulation from an outside source is not necessary for your body. If you are providing good fuels for your body, it will be able to create all of the energy your system requires. A common thought is that caffeine is a quick energy booster. This form of energy is extremely short-lived and can also place great stress on the adrenal system and cortisol levels in your body. Caffeine consumption leads to a rise in the cortisol levels in the body, and the stress cycle is then revved up. Your system stays revved up for as long as the stimulus is present. The problem is that caffeine is a simple fuel and is metabolized very quickly. When the caffeine is broken down in the body and is metabolized, this is when the crash occurs because the stimulus is no longer present. Have you ever experienced jitters when you have consumed too much coffee? This is the adrenal system being revved up beyond its normal capacity. This is your fight and flight response being engaged, but you are not running anywhere. Your blood pressure increases, as well as your heart rate. When this type of stimulus is provided on a regular basis, your system continues to function at this elevated rate and is never given the chance to come back to a resting idle. It is essential for your body to come back to a resting state on a very regular basis. The human body is not designed to function at high levels on a continuous basis or for extended periods of time. When you are at rest, restoration throughout your body happens. Every single moment that you are awake, your body is degenerating. Energy is being produced, waste products are being collected and excreted, cellular breakdown is happening, and you are deteriorating. While you sleep, these processes are being reversed. Even the word restoration begins with the word 'rest.' Your body has the opportunity to be restored while you are resting. Cellular repair happens when you sleep, and you are re-energized for the next day. This cycle is vital for your health and well-being. When your engine is continuously revved up and not given the opportunity to come back to rest, then this is when your parts start to wear out.

This is how consuming caffeine actually decreases your energy levels. I will be sharing with you, in upcoming chapters, much better sources of fuel for your body which will also prevent this crash and burn cycle from occurring.

6- Why Diets Don't Work

It is not your fault if you feel like you have failed while attempting to lose weight while on a weight-loss diet program. In actual fact if you have found yourself in this situation you can truly celebrate, because this means that your body was working very effectively at maintaining your body composition and ensuring your survival. This is a very good thing.

As I have shared with you in previous chapters, the sole purpose of all of the systems in your body is to ensure your survival. This is why you have a satiation centre, a reward cascade, and adaptation mechanisms, just to name a few. All of these systems, plus many others, are built right in to the amazing mechanism of your body, in order to ensure your survival. Without survival and reproduction the species would cease to exist. Without these mechanisms in place there would be grave consequences, and because the continuation of our species relies on this, these systems are very difficult to circumvent. Again, it is not your fault if you feel like you were not successful with your previous weight loss journey.

Here is the answer you have been looking for.

Diets do not work because your body has the miraculous ability to adapt. Period.

Diets do not work because your body has the ability to adapt to whatever you provide for it. For example, if you are in the Arctic, your body will shiver in response to this new environment, and the shivering will create energy to keep you warm. This is a survival mechanism. When you find yourself in a scary situation, your heart rate will increase rapidly, your blood pressure will increase, your breathing will increase, all in order for your body to be able to deliver the required oxygen and nutrients to your muscles so that you can run away as fast as possible. This is a survival mechanism. When you find yourself in a situation where your body is being deprived of food, it will hold on to every single morsel you put into your mouth. This too is a survival mechanism.

With dieting for weight loss, when you change what you are providing for your body, it will adapt to this new environment. With dieting, you end up following rules and guidelines and then restrict what you are providing for your body. Over a short period of time you will see results initially, but as your body begins to adapt to this new situation this is when your weight loss will plateau. The issue does truly lie with the survival mechanisms of your body. When you are depriving yourself, or skipping meals, your body becomes uncertain as to when the next meal will show up. Therefore it goes into starvation mode and it holds on to every single morsel that you eat. Another factor that comes into play is the reward cascade. When you are on a weight loss diet and you feel like you have been eating the stupid salads all week, it goes without saying that you worked really hard and now you deserve a reward. This reward cascade is hardwired into your system, and this is where your cheat days come in and sabotage all of your healthy living efforts from the entire week. Unfortunately the reward cascade is not generally satisfied by doing something that is healthy for you. Remember that the reward cascade is directly tied to the addiction centre and satiation centres in the brain, and this is where you end up being at the mercy of your cravings.

When you begin to incorporate healthy, natural choices into your lifestyle, as I discuss in further chapters in this book, this becomes not a diet of depravation, but a life filled with nourishment, freedom, and success. I will share with you exactly what your body does with what you give it, and from here you will be able to make informed choices as to what goals you want to achieve. I will also help you outline the steps you need in order to reach your goals.

When you begin to provide clean burning fuels for your engine, it will run more efficiently, and improved metabolism and weight loss will be the result. To take this to a deeper level I invite you to visit http://BalancedLivingAcademy.com and see what is possible for you.

When, If Not Now?

Record Your W.I.N.N.s Here

_____

_____

_____

_____

_____

_____

_____

_____

_____

_____

_____

_____

_____

_____

_____

_____

_____

_____

_____

_____

_____

_____

Chapter 5

Why Water

You are not a drop in the ocean.
You are the entire ocean, in a drop.
—Rumi

1-The Composition Of Your Body

If you recall from Chapter 3, I shared with you the importance of water for your body. One of the most critical components that your body requires is water, as it is only able to survive for three days without water. The reason for this is that every single system, organ and cell require water for all of their functions.

At this point I expect that you have taken some time to reflect on how much water you consume in a day. Have you started to make a conscious effort to increase the amount of water that you drink in a day? Have you thought about some of the things which you can begin to eliminate from your lifestyle in order to help reduce the water that is removed from your body every day? These are just two easy steps that you can begin to implement right now in order for your body to begin to function better. For easy ways to implement these two steps be sure to review the 2 part video series "Eliminate Your Hidden Energy Drainers™" which is easily found at www.DrStaceyCooper.com.

On average, the human body contains approximately 37.2 trillion cells, and is made up of 70 to 75% water. Your brain content is 83% water, your blood and eyes are 95% water, your kidneys and lungs 83%

water, your skeleton is 31% water, and your muscles including your heart muscle is 75% water.

Water in your body has many essential functions. It is a vital nutrient to the life and existence of every single cell. It acts first as a building material for every component in your body. Water is also a key factor in regulating your internal body temperature. When you are outdoors and exposed to rising temperatures, your body responds by excreting water onto your skin. Sweating is the mechanism which prevents your body from overheating.

Water is also a key component of the transportation system throughout your body. The carbohydrates and proteins that your body uses as fuel for energy production are transported by water in the bloodstream, and are then metabolized. Water is also crucial in excreting the waste products which were created during energy production. Water assists in flushing out waste products mainly through urination, but also through your skin when you sweat and your lungs when you exhale.

Another critical role that water plays is that of shock absorber. Your brain and spinal cord are housed inside your skull and your spine respectively. These bones are designed to protect the computer of your body. Of course you know that the bones are hard and rigid but the brain and spinal cord are very soft. During a traumatic injury if there was no water surrounding and cushioning this essential organ, it would be like dropping an egg on the floor. The yolk would splatter. However, if you were to drop an egg into a bucket of water which was placed on the floor, the egg would remain intact. It is cushioned by the water in the bucket. The same holds true for your brain inside of your skull. During quick impact movements the cerebral spinal fluid provides shock absorption and helps to protect your brain. This same mechanism holds true for the protection of a developing fetus. As babies develop, they are surrounded by amniotic fluid which also provides cushioning and shock absorption.

Another very vital function of water in your body is that it forms the saliva necessary for you to be able to chew, swallow and digest your food.

Water in the body is also essential for lubrication of all of your joints. Without water, you would not be able to move very well at all.

These are just some of the reasons why water is so vital for your existence and why you can only survive for 3 days without water.

2-It Is Essential For Cellular Function

Water is essential for every single cell to function properly. Hydration plays a very big role, and will also affect the flow through your entire digestive system. Therefore, it is very important to stay well hydrated. Your body requires approximately 2 litres of water every day. If you are dehydrated, your body will conserve every single drop of water you give it. The last place your body can absorb water from is the large intestine. When you have a negative water balance, meaning that you are consuming less water than what your body needs, the result will be constipation. The stool in your bowel will become dry and hard, and its journey through your digestive tract will be slowed down. This means that the waste products in your elimination systems will stay in your body longer and continue to release toxins back into your body for a longer period of time. This does not lead to improved health but rather creates a greater burden on your system. As these toxins seep back into your body, they have to be filtered from your blood and your tissues all over again, which will utilize more energy, and the toxins will actually become more concentrated as well. This whole scenario is a large energy drainer and will also inhibit your metabolic rate. This can create difficulties and great frustration when weight loss is a goal.

Another region that your body can also draw water from is your bladder. This is why your urine becomes darker in colour, more cloudy, and stronger in odour during times of low water intake. Another important fact to remember is that urine is very corrosive to the bladder wall. Therefore to maintain the health of your bladder, and your body, it is important to stay well hydrated and keep your systems well flushed out by consuming adequate amounts of water.

Water is also a solvent in your body because it helps to break down nutrients and waste products inside each cell. They can then be moved through the various membranes and natural filters throughout your body and metabolized and excreted. Without water none of these processes would be able to occur.

The source of water that you consume will have a huge effect on how your body will function due to the intimate involvement that water has with almost every single process that occurs inside of your body. You may be very fortunate to have access to a direct source of water in your home, whether that be from a well, a municipal water system, or a delivery service. Here is where the taste of water, as well as its quality, can be one of the main concerns.

I am very fortunate that I was raised in the countryside of St. George, Ontario, and my water supply came from a natural artesian well. I remember when I would visit my grandmother and Baba in the city, and even as a young child I knew that I disliked the horrible chlorine smell of the city water and I never drank it, as I could not get it past my nose. The city water, of course, came from a water treatment plant where the water had been processed and presumably made fit for human consumption. The issue again, as with processed foods, is that as the water is processed, it has been tampered with, filtered, and chemicals have also been added. Did you know that your body is not designed to ingest fluoride or chlorine?

Fluoride has been shown to prevent cavities when applied to the surface of teeth, but it should never be ingested and certainly not consumed via the water supply. Fluoride is known to impact the cardiovascular, central nervous, digestive, endocrine, immune, integumentary, renal, respiratory, and skeletal systems, and exposure to fluoride has been linked to Alzheimer's disease, cancer, diabetes, heart disease, infertility, and many other adverse health outcomes.

Chlorine is used as a disinfectant and can be described as a pesticide whose sole purpose is to cause damage to living organisms. Chlorine is used to kill waterborne pathogens, among other things. Chlorine cannot differentiate between what is a pathogen and what is part of the normal flora of your healthy gut micro biome, and drinking water contaminated with chlorine leads to the destruction of cells and tissues inside your body just as it destroys pathogens. This explains the carcinogenic behaviour of chlorine and its link to bladder cancer.

There have now been municipalities that have mentioned in their water quality reports the possible health risk for people that have undergone organ transplants, for cancer patients on certain drugs, some elderly people, infants, and people with HIV Aids or other immune system disorders, from drinking municipal water. (This warning comes from the U.S. Environmental Protection Agency and is effective for all municipal water systems.)

If water is the second most vital component that the body needs, only to come second after air, if the municipal water supply actually delivers more chemicals to the body, and water quality reports cite a possible health risk from drinking the municipal water, then what is a person to do? Even with good health, I know that I don't want to challenge my immune system every time I go to the tap for a drink of water. This is why I prefer to enjoy restructured alkaline water. I will share more about this with you in the following sections.

3-The Effects Of Diuretics

When it comes to hydrating your body, not all fluids are created equal. Some are absorbed more readily than others, while some actually remove water from your system. These are called diuretics. Examples of these water-depleting substances are caffeinated beverages and alcohol. The right sources of hydration for your body are important in keeping energy production at optimal levels.

The right source of hydration is water, and water is truly all your body needs, as long as you are consuming a balanced diet. A point to remember here is that there are many sources of water and these too are not all created equal. Water for hydrating your body is simple; it does not require complicated processing, and it is absorbed readily. In order to reach optimal hydration levels, as a general guideline you should try to drink between half an ounce and an ounce of water for each pound you weigh. This may seem like a lot at first, but your system will quickly balance out to your new water load. From a scientific standpoint there is an easy way to determine the hydration level of your body as I discussed in Chapter 3. This is the "P" test. When your body is well hydrated your urine will be clear, colourless, and odourless. As a side note, urine is acidic, and the more concentrated it becomes, the more corrosive it is to the bladder wall. For good bladder health it is important to keep well hydrated. Your bowel function will also be improved when you are well hydrated. With dehydration comes constipation, and with constipation comes many other issues, so be sure to improve your bowel health by increasing your water intake. Now let's explore some other options for hydrating your body. Coffee, tea, beer, wine, liquor and soda pops are all examples of diuretics and lead to dehydration of the body.

Alcohol contributes to dehydration in two different ways. First, alcohol acts on the kidneys in such a way that it leads to an increase in urine output, which is greater than the amount of fluids that you have consumed. This is what causes a negative water balance and leads to dehydration. Secondly, alcohol also reduces the production of a hormone called vasopressin. This hormone tells your kidneys to reabsorb water. When vasopressin levels are decreased, your kidneys do not reabsorb water back into your body, and this allows all of the fluids to flush out through the bladder, and also contributes to dehydration.

Caffeine has two different effects on your body, but still leads to increased urine output and a negative water balance. First, your bladder is just like a water balloon and it is made up of muscle. The detrusor muscles in your bladder help to determine the capacity limits of the bladder. They also control your bladder output into the urethra when you are urinating. The first effect of caffeine from coffee, tea, and colas is that it relaxes the detrusor muscles in your bladder, thereby causing the bladder to feel fuller more frequently. This results in you having to make more frequent trips to the bathroom. The second effect of caffeine is that it causes the bladder to be incapable of holding larger amounts of urine, causing you an urgency to urinate. This indirectly compounds the diuretic effects of caffeine.

I know these mechanisms may seem complicated to understand. Your body is a very complex mechanism with intricate workings where each system depends upon another, and nothing happens in isolation. As we explore the intricacies of these mechanisms you will be able to understand how fuelling your body differently will lead to new and improved outcomes as you reach for your healthy living goals.

Becoming more conscious of your choices for hydrating your body will lead to an improvement in your body function, resulting in enhanced energy production at the cellular level. This will progress to improved metabolism and lead to effortless weight loss and enhanced vitality naturally.

4-The Importance of pH Balance

The concept of pH and alkalinity were initially confusing for me, and the first thing I would like you to know is that pH and alkalinity are not the same thing.

Water pH measures the amount of hydrogen H^+ (acid ions) in the water, whereas water alkalinity is a measure of water's buffering capacity to neutralize acids. Alkalinity is the measure of the carbonate and bicarbonate levels in water, and its ability to resist changes in pH upon the addition of acids or bases.

pH is a measure of how acidic/alkaline water is. The pH scale ranges from 0 - 14, with 7 being neutral. pH of less than 7 indicates acidity, whereas a pH of greater than 7 indicates alkalinity. pH is really a measure of the relative amount of free hydrogen (H^+) and hydroxyl ions (OH^-) in the water. Water that has more free H^+ is acidic, whereas water that has more free OH^- is basic. Since pH can be affected by chemicals in the water, pH is an important indicator of water that is changing chemically. pH is measured on a logarithmic scale, therefore each number on the pH scale represents a 10-fold change in the acidity/alkalinity of the water. Water with a pH of 5 is ten times more acidic than water having a pH of 6, while a pH of 4 is 100 times more acid that a pH of 6.

Did you know that your body has its own natural chemistry lab? It creates hormones, digestive enzymes, neurotransmitters, cell communicators, and molecular carriers for transportation throughout the body. When you think of a swimming pool, you know that if the pH of the pool is not balanced, the chemicals will not work well. The same is true for your body. The pH of the bloodstream determines the wellness and balance of the body. If the pH is not balanced, the digestive enzymes cannot function at their optimal level, even though you may be providing fabulous fuels for your body. If your body's pH is not balanced, the fuels you provide for your body may just be exiting out the other end if they are not able to be broken down and absorbed first. This can result in nutrient deficiencies.

When foods are metabolized they leave behind a residue in your body. Some foods leave an acidic residue while others leave an alkaline residue. This is what affects blood pH. If your pH is not balanced, your enzymes, hormones and neurotransmitters cannot function optimally. You can manage your blood pH balance through the food you eat and the water you drink.

The North American diet is extremely acidic, and leads to the progression of many degenerative disease processes. These degenerative diseases can be reversed when you change the environment that you provide for your body. It is possible to heal your health naturally from within.

The human body has a neutral pH of 7.4. Your body needs to maintain this pH level to run efficiently and your body always seeks to return to this state. If your body becomes overly acidic or alkaline it will not function well, and it will strive to return to this balance point.

Drinking water that has had the minerals removed, such as filtered and reverse osmosis waters, along with eating acidic foods, can temporarily take your body out of balance.

5-The Importance Of Alkalinity

As I mentioned, alkalinity is a chemical measurement of water's ability to neutralize acids. Alkalinity is also a measure of water's buffering capacity, or its ability to resist changes in pH upon the addition of acids or bases. This capacity is caused by the water's content of carbonate, bicarbonate, hydroxide and occasionally borate, silicate and phosphate.

Natural water which passes over rocks, such as that which flows from a spring, is naturally alkaline because it picks up minerals as it travels over the rocks, and this increases its alkaline level. This water is of greatest value to your body and is the ultimate source; however, it is not always readily available. This is why I choose to drink restructured alkaline water.

A study published by the World Health Organization cautions against drinking water with low mineral content on a regular basis. Water with low mineral content is created by processes such as reverse-osmosis, distillation, and other methods when they do not incorporate additional mineralization. You know that your body requires vitamins as well as minerals in order to function well, and natural water is a source of minerals that your body can utilize.

There are a few studies that suggest alkaline water might be helpful for certain conditions. A 2012 study found that drinking naturally carbonated artesian-well alkaline water with a pH of 8.8 may help deactivate pepsin, the main enzyme that causes acid reflux.

Another study suggested that drinking alkaline ionized water may have benefits for people who have high blood pressure, diabetes, and high cholesterol.

A more recent study that included 100 people found a significant difference in whole blood viscosity (how easily the blood flows) after consuming high pH water compared to regular water after a strenuous workout. Those who consumed high pH water reduced viscosity by 6.3 percent compared to 3.36 percent with standard purified drinking water. This means that the blood flowed more efficiently in the subjects who consumed the alkaline water. This can increase oxygen delivery throughout the body, which of course will lead to increased energy production and therefore improved metabolism.

Proposed health benefits of alkaline water include: anti-aging properties (via liquid antioxidants that absorb more quickly into the human body); colon-cleansing properties; immune system support; hydration, skin health, and other detoxifying properties; weight loss and cancer resistance.

The typical North American diet is extremely acidic for the body to consume. Alkaline water is said to help counteract the acid that is found in your bloodstream. It is thought that drinking water with a higher pH can increase your metabolism and improve your body's ability to absorb vital nutrients. Of course with increased metabolism comes weight loss.

Some researchers have theorized that alkaline water will also starve any cancer cells found in your body because cancer cells thrive in an acidic environment, and if the acidic environment is alkalized then cancer cannot thrive.

In general, alkaline water may have a hydrating effect on your body and it might also improve symptoms related to stomach acid reflux. However, in a body with normal function, alkaline water sold at stores to the general public will not cause a significant change in your body's overall acid-base balance as measured in the bloodstream. This is why I choose to drink restructured alkaline Kangen Water®

6-What Is Re-Structured Water?

There are many different types of water available, and not all water hydrates the body efficiently. Take distilled water for example. This water has been termed "dead water" as it is devoid of all minerals. Minerals are an essential component of your body and are required from your diet. Water that has been stripped of its minerals is not a form of life-giving water. It is very acidic and will tend to actually dehydrate you.

All distilled waters measures about a 4.5pH. This means that this water is 1000 times more acidic than your blood, which is a 7.4pH. When you drink distilled water it must be neutralized in order for your body to maintain the point of homeostasis that it is always trying to achieve. What do you think your body will do in order to accomplish this? Your body is very resourceful and it has many mechanisms at its disposal. When your body is in an acidic state, it will actually pull minerals (calcium) from your bones in order to buffer the acid. This of course leads to weakening of the skeletal structure and increases the incidence of osteoporosis and fractures.

Reverse osmosis water has many of the same problems as I have just discussed. "RO Water" averages a 5pH and this is still 100 times more acidic than your blood, and therefore it will need to be buffered by your body as well.

As an alternative, restructured alkaline water can range from 8pH to 9.5pH. As you can see, this is past the neutral point on the pH scale, and this water does not place an acidic load on your body. It is actually at a higher pH than the blood, thereby relieving the stress on the body to keep your blood pH balanced.

Most health problems, including cancer, begin in an acid environment inside the body. What you may not be aware of is that if your pH does drop below 5.8 you cannot absorb the vitamins A, B, E, F and K and you cannot absorb valuable minerals like sulphur, potassium, calcium, vanadium, chromium, iron or zinc, no matter how much of these minerals you take. Think about it, you may be thinking that you are providing the right nutrients for your body but they may not be absorbed as you expect and therefore your money is literally going down the toilet. The majority of people have a urine pH below 5.8 and don't realize they are wasting their money on supplements. Restructured alkaline water is the fastest and most efficient way to alkalize your body. We are meant to be alkaline on the inside of our bodies. If you have any doubts about this I suggest you read "Alkalize or Die" by Dr. Theodore A. Baroody, available in most health stores.

Restructured alkaline water, made using electrolysis, has smaller clusters of molecules that enable it to hydrate you faster than tap water. It also carries nutrients and oxygen to your cells more efficiently, and removes acidic cellular waste with greater effectiveness. Premature aging in the body, as a result of the damage created by free radicals, is also slowed down with restructured alkaline water. Free radicals are renegade molecules which cause your body to oxidize on the inside. An example of this is when you slice open an apple and leave it exposed to the air, and it turns brown. The apple is being oxidized right before your eyes, and this leads to deterioration of the tissue. It is not a good thing when oxidization happens inside your body because this leads to the deterioration of your tissues. You can actually see some of this kind of damage in the form of excess wrinkles on the outside of your body as the collagen tissue in your skin begins to break down and degenerate. In order to slow down oxidization, antioxidants are required. Restructured alkaline water is a powerful antioxidant and is loaded with additional negative electrons that can be used by your body to neutralize free radicals. Drinking restructured alkaline water can relieve or reduce the three main causes for sickness, disease and premature aging by improving the alkalinity of your body, reducing oxidation of your tissues, and improving your levels of hydration. It can be as easy as going to your kitchen counter and filling up a glass of healthy, good tasting water, that is also one of the best antioxidants you could put in your body. In each glass full of restructured alkaline water you can hydrate your body, build a stronger immune system, alkalize your body and slow down degenerative diseases, all at the same time.

Of course it is not just the water that you drink that affects the pH of your blood, but also the food that you eat. Food, as it is being broken down, will either leave behind an acidic residue for an alkaline residue in the blood, and this too must be buffered by the body. When you consume foods that leave behind an acidic residue and you are drinking restructured alkaline water, you are solving half the battle when trying to provide an environment which resists the development of inflammation, degenerative diseases and even cancer. In Chapter 8 I will share with you how to swap out acidic forming foods as well.

Restructured alkaline water made using electrolysis has been consumed by the Japanese for over 40 years, and has touched and changed every disease and condition imaginable. I have been using this water and have seen similar results when it is used persistently and consistently. The water is delicious, hydrating, energizing, permeating, pH balancing and a very strong antioxidant. This is why I choose to drink restructured alkaline Kangen Water®. For more information please email me at drstacey@drstaceycooper.com with the subject: Water.

In chapter 3 I discussed the essential components that your body needs in order to function well. However, there are many different food sources which will fall into the categories of water, protein, fats and carbohydrates, and not all of those things are good for your body. In the next chapter I will talk about what happens on the inside when you eat certain foods. With this understanding of metabolization in your body, and when you know what direction you want to go with your health, you will be able to make your choices so much easier. I will also share with you how to swap out the bad fuels for great nourishing whole food sources.

When, If Not Now?

Record Your W.I.N.N.s Here

_____
_____
_____
_____
_____
_____
_____
_____
_____
_____
_____
_____
_____
_____
_____
_____
_____
_____
_____

Chapter 6

What Your Body Does With What You Give It

Eliminating the things you love is not wellness.
Wellness feeds your soul and makes you feel good.
— Iman

1-Food Provides Messages To Your Cells

Do you take much time in your day to think about what happens to the things that you eat once they are inside your body? Did you know that the food you eat provides messages and sends signals to your cells, as well as providing the building blocks for development, repair, regeneration and energy production?

Food plays a very important role in the health of your body, and a lot of time is spent eating, multiple times in a day. Many social activities also revolve around food. Eating is exciting. It involves the senses of sight, taste, touch, and smell. It is social and it is not optional. It is something that you need to do regularly, every single day, in order to achieve optimal health. The question is how to do it in such a fashion that you are truly nourishing your body naturally.

The food you provide for your body dictates how communication between cells occurs, how hormones interact, and how neurotransmitters will function. This all occurs through positive and negative messages. Here again is where you can change the environment that you are providing for your body and thereby change your outcomes. It is possible to have your body experience improved function by providing healthy fuels which then relay positive messages to all of your cells.

Your body is truly a remarkable mechanism, and every bite of food that you ingest provides messages and sends signals to every single cell, which alters their function. The issue is that it is not only positive messages which are provided for your body, but some foods send negative messages too. As discussed earlier, not all sources of fuel for your body are created or utilized equally. Just as some foods leave behind an acidic residue, others leave behind an alkaline residue. Some fluids are much better at hydrating your body than others, and some foods satisfy your satiation centre better than others. Unfortunately these negative messages are not something that you can just exercise away because it is not just calories that you want to burn off; if you are not fuelling your body well, those negative messages cannot just be erased with exercise because the function of the cell has actually been altered. These negative messages will affect the cell at a molecular level and change the functioning of the cell. This of course, will negatively affect the function of your entire body.

Another factor to consider is that when healthy nutrients are not provided for your body, when it experiences a stressor it cannot adapt and meet that challenge as effectively. In this case even exercise would become a negative stressor to your body rather than be a health benefit. If your body is in starvation mode, there is no fuel available for exercise. This is how it now becomes a negative stressor.

The long-term effects of fuelling your body poorly can be seen when examining the state of the healthcare system. The effect is costing trillions of dollars. There are increased office visits for ill health conditions, prescribed medications, costly investigations, ultrasound examinations, MRI and CT scans, invasive procedures and hospital stays. When you fuel your body well, your cost to the healthcare system is very low. The key is prevention.

In order to provide positive messages for the cells of your body, it is best to eat many varieties of plant-based food in order to provide balanced nutrition. This includes eating all the colours of the rainbow. Different coloured foods provide a feast for the eyes, but also provide different nutrients for the body. You may know that carrots contain bcarotene which is important for eye health. Each vegetable has different nutrients that your body needs. When choosing whole fresh foods to fill your plate with, be sure to select many different colours. This will entice your eyes and taste buds, but also provide you with the balance in vitamins, minerals and nutrients that your body needs.

2-The Role Of Enzymes

In Chapter 4 I illustrated the complexity of your digestive system. Once food has made its way to your stomach, digestion has already begun, as you have digestive enzymes present in your saliva even as you are chewing your food. In the stomach the gastric juices begin to work their magic so that the food stuff you ingested can be broken down into its elemental pieces which can then be used by your body for growth, development, maintenance, repair and energy production.

Your body is equipped with digestive enzymes to break down only foods of the earth. This is what nature intended, and there are no exceptions. You are not equipped to break down things which were produced in a laboratory. This is why additives, preservatives and anything artificial cannot be digested by your body, and leads to an increase in the toxic load of your systems. Any food stuff which is processed, packaged and manufactured is of very little nutritional benefit. All high heat processing leads to the destruction of the healthy nutrients, vitamins, and minerals which had been present in the ingredients prior to processing. If it comes in a box, can, or package and has a label with ingredients that you don't recognize and cannot pronounce, don't eat it. Your body will not gain much nutritional benefit from it.

The first stage of digestion takes place in the mouth as you begin to chew your food, which starts the breakdown of starches. In the stomach you have the next stage, where the acidic juices enhance digestion and the breakdown of the food into smaller particles. As the food moves down your system there are enzymes released from the gallbladder for fat emulsification and there are also alkaline secretions from the pancreas to continue further digestion in the small intestines. Many processes need to happen in order for digestion to go to completion. If the pH of the body is not balanced, these processes cannot work efficiently, nutrients will not be broken down readily, and they will be voided without being absorbed. The result can be nutrient deficiencies.

Once foods are broken down into their molecular pieces, absorption can occur across membranes. Absorption occurs in the stomach, and in the small and large intestines. This is where the nutrients will be picked up from the digestive system and delivered, via the blood and circulatory system, to every single cell within the rest of the body. If the cells are unhealthy in the digestive system, absorption cannot occur via these structures.

The speed with which your food travels through your digestive system is affected by many factors. If it passes too quickly through the system, nothing can be absorbed. Sometimes this is a good thing. In the case of food poisoning you do not want any of that bad toxic stuff remaining in your body, so your body ushers it out as fast as possible. The body is a remarkable adaptive mechanism and is always looking out for survival of the fittest. It is important to let the body do its job. When you interfere with this process, by taking something like Immodium, for example, you are slowing down the healing and restorative processes of the body and you are keeping the toxins in longer. What do you think is better for your system?

When you provide healthy plant-based, colourful foods which are not processed or packaged, and are not full of preservatives and chemicals, your body can digest, absorb and utilize these healthy fuels and begin to experience enhanced function.

3-Proteins

As I shared with you in Chapter 3, protein is one of the most abundant compounds in the body. It is an essential element of the body, as every organ and cell is composed of protein. There are also many chemical reactions in the body which are dependant on proteins because enzymes and hormones are made up of proteins. Because protein is utilized in so many ways throughout your entire body, it is necessary at every single meal in order to keep up with the demand. In order to ensure the best start to your day protein is vital at breakfast in order to clear brain fog.

My smoothies, which are from the Healthy Smoothie Blueprint™, are the easiest way that I have found to fulfill all of the nutritional requirements — protein, fats, and complex fuels - for my body. I have them first thing in the morning, and this sustains me to lunchtime because it is a complex fuel.

When you consume a muffin and coffee from the drive-through, all of this is highly refined and processed and it is a simple fuel. With my smoothies I add whole fruits and vegetables and since these are complex fuels it will take longer for the digestive system to process and metabolize. This is why I do not experience the crash and burn cycle at 10:00am. To review the Crash and Burn cycle, see Chapter 4.

Protein is not just found in meat products. Plants also have protein. Animal proteins are now domesticated and manufactured rather than obtained from nature. The animals are fed a diet that is far from what they were intended to eat naturally. In nature, cows graze in pastures and gain their sustenance from grasses. In the manufacturing of animal proteins, cattle are now kept in feed lots and fed grain. Since the animals are now being fed a diet that is not natural to them, their bodies have to utilize these building blocks in a different fashion, and the resulting meat is not the same as that which is developed when a cow is allowed to graze on their natural diet of grass. So if you ingest this manufactured meat protein your body does not recognize it to be the same as that which was enjoyed by your ancestors, and it has to find a way to assimilate this new protein. Now this altered protein source is being consumed by your body, and this changes how your body utilizes it, resulting in a different outcome. If you choose to consume meat products, then grass-fed, natural grazing beef is a better choice.

On a worldwide basis, plant protein foods contribute over 60% of the per capita supply of protein on average. In North America, animal derived foods contribute about 70% of the protein sources. For the whole rest of the world 60% of their protein comes strictly from plants. When you look at the incidence of obesity in North America, do you think something has gone wrong?

Let's now look at the physical anatomy of your body. Every single aspect of our physical design is suited for a specific purpose. The same is true for every type of creature that walks this earth. It truly is remarkable when you consider the diversity of organisms and creatures and how unique each of them is. This includes every single aspect of their being from how their eyes are positioned on their head, how their ears move, what shape their teeth are, and how they use their limbs. This holds true for humans as well.

When you think about an animal that eats meat, a lion for example, think about the type of teeth they have. Lions have teeth that are spaced apart, are sharp and pointy, and are used for tearing meat. Animals that eat plants and grasses such as cows, horses or gorillas, have front teeth that meet together so that they can rip grass from the ground, and they have flat back teeth for grinding the plant material.

Did you ever think about your teeth and what they were designed for? Are human teeth large and pointy and spaced apart? Or are they positioned in such a manner that the teeth meet together in the front and that the back molars are flat for grinding?

When you also delve into the structure and length of the different segments of the digestive system of different animals, as well as the acidity of the stomach enzymes and juices, it is very evident that the digestive system of meat eaters varies greatly from that of plant eaters.

Here I have outlined for you just a few of the anatomical and physiological reasons why animal sources of protein are not the best protein for your body. I invite you to further explore this subject as it is beyond the intent of this particular book.

Legumes are one of the best sources of plant proteins, with quinoa being the only complete protein from a plant source. Legumes are a more complete protein than whole grains and cereals. Whole grains and cereals are incomplete proteins, as they tend to be limited in the amino acid lysine or threonine, which is available in other plant sources. This is why it is important to combine plant sources of proteins so that you get the full complement of all of the amino acids every day.

Vegans get enough essential amino acids by eating a variety of plant proteins and by combining them. If you do not eat animal products, it is important to eat different types of plant foods together or within the same day to get the proper balance and amount of essential amino acids that your body requires. Combining beans and rice, lentils and barley, or nut butter and steel cut wheat-free oats will provide all of the essential amino acids in the right amounts. These food combinations mix foods from different plant groups to complement the amino acids provided by each. Combining foods from any two of the following plant groups will provide a higher quality protein.

For your convenience I have provided a list for easy reference.

- Legumes - beans, peas, lentils, kidney beans, white beans, mung beans, chickpeas, cowpeas, lima beans, pigeon peas, and lupines
- Nuts - almonds, brazil nuts, cashews, walnuts, hazelnuts, pecans, and pistachios
- Seeds - cotton, pumpkin, sesame, sunflower, chia, flax, and hemp hearts
- Fruits - dried apricots, raisins, guava, dates, prunes, avocado, kumquat, jackfruit, currants, raspberries, bananas, peaches, figs, grapefruit, and cantaloupe
- Grains - buckwheat, steel cut oats, millet, rice, sorghum, amaranth, and quinoa

Provide for your body a variety of complex fuels from a variety of sources, including all of the colours of the rainbow, in order to ensure balanced nutrition and optimal functioning of your body and enhanced vitality.

4-Fats

It may seem counterintuitive to you that I suggest that a great fuel for the body is fat, when I expect that you may have heard many times, either from the media or even from your medical doctor, that consuming a low-fat diet is a healthy idea. Many are under the assumption that eating fat makes us fat. I am here to dispel this myth and let you know what happens physiologically inside your body when you eat a low-fat diet.

Eating fat does not make you fat. Eating sugar and starches is what makes you fat. You have learned that fats are an essential component of every single cell membrane (Chapter 3). A low-fat diet consists of food products which have had the fat removed. The problem lies in the fact that, once the fat has been removed, it no longer tastes good, and in order for it to taste good sugar has been added. It is now the sugar that is making you fat!

As the fat content is decreased in low-fat diets, a greater portion of the food product is being made up of animal protein. These low-fat/high-protein animal products lead to a rapid increase in the incidence of cancer.

Starving your body of fat actually leads to a breakdown in the neurological function of your brain and nervous system, and results in the progression of degenerative diseases. Without a functioning brain the body cannot survive. Therefore consuming a low-fat diet is not healthy at all.

Eating healthy dietary fats is essential for optimal function of your body, and they are utilized for many purposes within your body. Fats are used for producing energy in your body, but even more importantly they are used to support cell growth. Many of the components of a cell are made up of fat, not to mention that the proper function of every cellular wall is dependent on components derived from fat molecules. If there is a deficiency of healthy fats, the cell walls will become weak and leaky, and then the function of the cell becomes compromised. This can lead to many deficiencies including vitamin deficiency within the body.

Fat in your body also helps to protect your organs. Just as water is important to provide cushioning and shock absorption to your brain, spinal cord, and joints, as well as to a developing fetus, fat is also important for providing cushioning and protection to your internal organs.

Another very important function of fat is as a source of energy, and to help keep your body warm. Did you know that your body has different kinds of fat? As an infant you had much more 'brown' fat, which works at a higher metabolic rate in order to keep you from being too cold. Unlike regular white fat which stores calories and energy in your body, the brown fat is packed with mitochondria which are the power generators of the cell. Therefore the brown fat cells are designed to burn energy and produce heat. This is of critical importance to infants. In babies, brown fat makes up about 5% of their body mass. It is located on their back, along the upper half of the spine and toward the shoulders. It is of great importance as its role is to prevent hypothermia, as lethal cold is a major death risk for premature neonates. The development of brown fat is another example of survival of the fittest.

Fats are also very important in helping your body absorb nutrients, including all of the fat-soluble vitamins, and also to produce important hormones.

As you can see, the consumption of healthy fats plays a critical role in keeping your body functioning at optimal levels. I invite you to continue to read on, as in later chapters I will also share with you how to swap out bad fats for great healthy fats.

5-Wheat

Wheat, when ingested, has many effects on the body. Not only is the Addiction Centre affected, as discussed in Chapter 4, but many systems are affected. Wheat is very inflammatory which contributes to the development of degenerative disease processes in the body.

By becoming wheat and gluten free this allows the body to eliminate the inflammation which was present, and healing can begin. With just 5 days of being wheat and gluten free you will notice changes in the functioning of your body. You may experience a decrease in intestinal bloating and abdominal upset, a decrease in heartburn, indigestion and acid reflux. You may also notice the lack of craving which occurs once you eliminate wheat and gluten from your diet. As months progress and you remain committed to excluding wheat and gluten from your lifestyle you will notice even more remarkable changes as your body begins to repair itself. These changes are the reversal of disease processes. Ill-health conditions and diseases can actually be reversed as the inflammation in the body is eliminated and healing can occur. I have patients who have experienced the reversal of celiac disease, colitis, Crohn's disease, liver disorders and cardiovascular disease. Over the course of years, chronic conditions such as multiple sclerosis, insulin dependent diabetes, and nutritional deficiencies can heal. Now this is not just me saying this; this is the research that Dr. William Davis has done, and what he has shared through the Wheat Belly Project.

Some of the issues that surround wheat are partly due to the fact that the wheat of today is not what it used to be. It has been genetically modified, and grows differently to enable easier harvesting, not to be more healthful for you the consumer. The manufacturing process also strips the wheat of any of its nutritional value as it is first milled, then highly refined and bleached into white flour.

Just as I have previously discussed simple fuels and how they are detrimental because they lead to spikes in blood sugar levels, wheat too is a simple fuel and does exactly the same thing. We talked about how the muffin from the drive-thru dissolves in your mouth quickly, enters your system, does not require a lot of chewing, and causes a lot of sugar to enter your system. White flour is also a simple fuel and floods your system with sugar, leading to the same problem of spiking blood sugar levels. Because the flour is so highly refined, when it is ingested it is immediately absorbed, which leads to the spike in blood sugar levels and then stresses the pancreas and leads to a spiking in insulin levels. This is the diabetic connection. I will discuss this mechanism further in the next section on sugar.

Eventually, a vicious circle of increased insulin resistance, increased insulin production, increased deposition of visceral fat, increased insulin resistance, etc., ensues. This is decreased body function.

Another issue with wheat is gluten. Gluten is the protein in the wheat. I would like to ask you to remember back to when you may have made pancakes, or any other batter containing wheat and a liquid. Perhaps you may have spilled the batter on the countertop and did not wipe it up right away. Remember when it dried like glue onto the countertop and had to then be chiseled off? This is due to the gluten.

It makes glue when mixed with a liquid. When you ingest this, it can coat the intestines with the glue and lead to a reduction in the absorption of the rest of the nutritious food you are providing for your body. The result can be malabsorption issues, as well as inflammation of your digestive tract.

Elimination of wheat can yield rapid weight loss due to the combination of halting the glucose-insulin-fat-deposition cycle as well as the natural reduction in cravings which leads to a reduced caloric intake.

Now you know the mechanism behind why wheat is the source of your cravings, why wheat is known as the comfort food, and you also know why it is harmful for your well-being. Are you ready to make a change, not by starting a diet but by creating a change in lifestyle? Let's connect now for your complimentary 30 minute discovery call and we can determine together where your next best steps will take you. I am here to help so just email me with subject: Next Steps at drstacey@drstaceycooper.com.

6-Sugars

Now with what I have shared with you so far, you know that sugar does not just come from sugary processed candy as you may have previously thought. Sugar has been added to many processed foods, with one of the largest sources being low-fat food products. The double whammy comes when you actually believe that you are doing something good for your body by providing low-fat choices, and in actual fact you are adding a lot of unwanted sugar instead.

As sugar becomes more refined, it is broken down into smaller and smaller particles. It is stripped of any fibre, healthful minerals or other nutrients. This is how it can easily dissolve when stirred into liquids. The same occurs when you ingest it. It is easily digested, rapidly released into the blood stream, and causes a severe spike in blood sugar levels. The same holds true for all simple fuels. They are detrimental because they lead to spikes in blood sugar levels.

As with many substances in the body, sugar too requires a carrier in order for it to be transported into liver cells and muscle tissue where it can be utilized for energy production. Insulin is the carrier for simple sugars. When you eat processed and refined foods, there is a rapid influx of sugar from these simple fuels into the bloodstream, and the pancreas, which produces the insulin, can become stressed and overworked. This can result in prolonged elevated blood sugar levels. This is a precursor to diabetes. When you swap out the simple fuels from your diet with complex fuels, this will no longer be a factor.

Did you know that you don't have to be a diabetic in order to experience high blood sugar and high insulin? Non-diabetics can easily experience high blood sugars, particularly because many foods, including those made from wheat, so readily convert to sugar. High blood insulin levels provoke the accumulation of abdominal fat as this is the body's means of storing excess energy. This abdominal fat then produces inflammatory signals in your body. As this system continues to spiral out of control, you end up with a decrease in the response of the muscles and the liver cells to the insulin, and this equals insulin resistance. Your body now says "Oh, my cells are not responding to the insulin, I better start making more insulin." This so-called insulin resistance means that the pancreas must produce greater and greater quantities of insulin in order to transport the sugar into the cells for metabolization. Eventually, a vicious circle of increased insulin resistance, increased insulin production, increased deposition of visceral fat, increased insulin resistance, etc., ensues. This is decreased body function. Please refer to the accompanying diagram depicting how high blood insulin contributes to increased deposition of abdominal fat on the next page.

Consumption of simple sugars leads to an elevation in levels of bad cholesterol, inflammation throughout the body, heart disease, and obesity. Our modern North American diets cause repeated insulin spiking, creating mood swings, cravings, hunger and weight gain. Our cells become resistant to insulin's action. More insulin must be made to keep blood sugar under control.

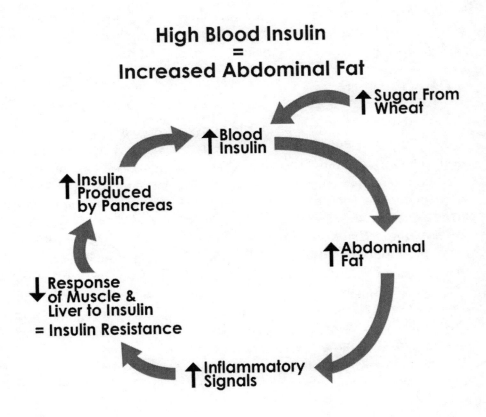

High Blood Insulin
=
Increased Abdominal Fat

Other syndromes associated with insulin resistance include but are not limited to: accelerated aging, acne, anxiety, asthma and eczema, elevated blood pressure, increased bad cholesterol, constipation, erectile dysfunction, fatigue, heartburn, heart disease, hypertension, arthritis and inflammation, low vitamin levels, male-pattern baldness, mental fuzziness, mood swings, need for stimulants, increased abdominal weight, pre-menstrual syndrome, depression, stroke, sleep disorders, and sugar cravings, just to name a few!

The good news is that this metabolic syndrome can be reversed. Here is the secret. It is not so much about controlling calories, but rather providing low-insulin-potential foods for your system, which will help you to decrease the load on your pancreas. You will then make less insulin, and will be able to use it more effectively. You will know when you are experiencing success when your cravings diminish, then disappear. This is when your healing will begin.

7-Dairy Products

As mammals, we produce milk to nourish our young. Mother's milk is by far the best nutrition for her infants. However, a consideration I would like you to explore is the fact that as a human, cows are not your mother. You know that your body is not designed to grow to the size of a cow in one year's time. So why is it that you are told by the media and advertising that drinking cow's milk is healthy for you? Do you see any other mammal that drinks another mammal's milk? A giraffe does not drink hippopotamus milk. So what are we doing drinking another mammal's milk? This same argument holds true for any other mammal's milk, whether it be goat's milk, horse milk or whale milk. Our bodies are not designed to do this. We cannot digest the protein in cow's milk. Why would we logically think it would be acceptable to consume milk from these other sources?

The next consideration is the weaning of young mammals. Every mammal goes through this normal stage of development, and they do not continue to drink their mother's milk once they have been weaned. Mother's milk is provided to offspring only during infancy, and it is necessary for proper growth and development during this time. Infants require the essential nutrients provided to them through their mother's milk in order to grow, flourish and thrive. During the weaning process the infant begins to consume the adult diet, and once this transition is complete they never go back to drinking milk from their mother. Do you ever see a mature mammal go back to its mother after being weaned and say "Hey Mom! I'm thirsty!"? Why is it that humans as children, teenagers, and adults consume the milk of a different mammal throughout their lifetime after being weaned from their own mother? Where is the logic here? Why do we drink milk? Because we were told to! Do you think there is some misinformation here that you have been led to believe?

Another common belief as to why dairy milk is important for the body has to do with calcium. Did you know that all whole foods contain the essential nutrient calcium, not just dairy products? The calcium found in dairy products is not absorbable by the body, as magnesium is not present in the milk. Adequate levels of magnesium are essential for the absorption and metabolization, not only of calcium, but of Vitamin D. Magnesium converts Vitamin D into its active form so that it can enable calcium to be absorbed by the body. When you consume your nutrients from plant-based whole food sources, your body receives all of the nutrients it requires. The uptake of nutrients into cells occurs normally, and the body is able to thrive.

As you may recall from earlier chapters, I discussed how some foods when they are metabolized will leave behind an acidic residue and some will leave an alkaline residue. Dairy products leave an acidic residue in the body once they are metabolized. In order for the body to balance the resulting rise in blood acidity, it will take calcium from your bones to buffer your blood. This leads to weakening of your skeleton, and the result is osteoporosis. It has been shown that the higher the rate of dairy consumption, the higher the risk of hip fractures, which is a prime indicator of osteoporosis. North America has the highest consumption of dairy products and the highest incidence of osteoporosis. So why is it that you are encouraged to consume dairy products, and what good does it do for your body?

I have shared with you in Chapter 3 what nutrients your body requires for optimal function, and here I have discussed what happens on the inside. In Chapter 8 I will show you how to swap out the bad fuels for great complex fuels in order to improve the function of your body. Next let's talk about healing your body from the inside out.

When, If Not Now?

Record Your W.I.N.N.s Here

Chapter 7

Reversing Disease Processes Naturally

Let food be thy medicine.
—Hippocrates

1-Obesity And Diabetes

Weight loss is common advice for a whole list of conditions from heart disease, high blood pressure, cholesterol, diabetes, obesity, sleep apnea, back pain, knee pain, joint pain, and arthritis, just to name a few. You may have been given a diagnosis and now you are truly concerned for your health. You have been told what needs to happen — you need to lose weight — but you have not been told how to do it. You may have been there before, trying different diets, and you are still not satisfied.

It can be so difficult to find the right information in regards to what you should be eating. The difficulty arises when most of your knowledge is gained through the media and advertising. You may know that Canada's Food Guide is taught in schools for the health curriculum in Canada, and there will be something similar in your local region as well. You may be familiar with the suggested food groups on the food guide. Are you familiar with who funds these documents? Even Canada's Food Guide is a form of advertising, as it is funded through the food manufacturing industries. There is a large segment of the population who want you to believe that this is how you should be feeding your body on a daily basis, and it is still being taught in our grade schools.

There is tremendous scientific evidence which supports the fact that

Canada's Food Guide does not nourish your body but is actually detrimental to your health, yet this is what hospital dieticians are mandated by the government to follow, and counsel their patients on. I know this to be true through experience with my patients and the medical system. It is no wonder you may feel confused and frustrated when it comes to knowing what is best for your health and well-being.[1]

Did you know that wheat increases blood sugar more than white table sugar? This fact may surprise you.

The Glycemic Index, (GI) is the measure of how much blood sugar levels increase in the 90-120 minutes after a food is consumed. The reason it is measured after 90-120 minutes is because digestion takes time. It takes time from when food enters your mouth, is chewed, swallowed, enters the stomach, is broken down by digestive enzymes, and then the carrier agents transport the molecules across the gut wall. Only after all of this do the glucose molecules begin to circulate in the blood stream. By this measure, whole wheat bread has a GI of 72, while plain table sugar has a GI of only 59. It is also very interesting to note that pulverized starches such as cornstarch, rice starch, potato starch, and tapioca starch all have a high glycemic index, and that these compounds are the basis of the manufacturing of gluten-free foods.

Did you know that you do not have to be a diabetic to experience high blood sugar and high insulin levels? Non-diabetics can easily experience high blood sugars, particularly because so many foods are made from wheat which so readily converts to sugar. High blood insulin provokes the accumulation of abdominal fat which of course results in obesity. The accumulation of abdominal fat is how your body stores excess energy. When visceral fat accumulates, this is the Wheat Belly (please refer back to the diagram on page 91— How High Blood Insulin Contributes to Abdominal Fat).

---

[1] The newest version of Canada's Food Guide, released on January 21, 2019, is a vast improvement over the 12 year old version I was referring to. Health Canada states that the food industry was not involved in the creation of the new version. The new guide recommends water as the drink of choice, and places greater emphasis on a plant-based diet, and I am in full agreement with this.

Now you can see the direct relationship between spiking blood sugar levels due to consuming a diet of refined wheat, sugar and processed foods, and that of increased abdominal visceral fat leading to obesity.

The food pyramid tells you to eat wheat-based foods as well as processed foods. I have shared with you that this is not what your body needs in order to function well. The food manufacturers have also created new food products, leading you to believe that you are making healthier choices when truly it will just make your system more taxed and lead to dysfunction and disease. With the information that is shared through the mainstream media, it may seem that you really can't win when it comes to breaking out of this system.

There is hope when you break free of the mainstream, get back to nature, and fuel your body as it was designed to function. Your body is remarkable, and can adapt to whatever environment that you provide.

All of the diseases which I listed at the beginning of this chapter are a result of degeneration of your system, and are just signs to let you know that your body is not functioning well. You can change the function of your body by changing the environment that you provide.

Type 2 diabetes is a condition that is characterized by chronically elevated blood sugar levels. However, the main cause as well as the driver for this condition is Insulin Resistance which I discussed in Chapter 6. When you eat certain foods, particularly refined carbohydrates, that food is converted to sugar inside your body. Your body's way of dealing with this sugar is to produce a hormone called insulin. Insulin is the carrier which moves the sugar into your cells so that it can be used for energy. The problem is that the effects of increased insulin levels are that it causes water and salt retention. Remember how I mentioned that nothing in the body happens in isolation? Well, this water and salt retention then causes blood pressure levels to increase. Now you become at risk of atherosclerosis, which can lead to heart attacks and death. But that is not where it ends. Increased insulin levels also elevate the VLDL level (very low density lipoprotein). This is one of the "bad" forms of cholesterol.

Insulin resistance can also cause ovaries in women to produce more testosterone, which is associated with Polycystic Ovarian Syndrome.

As you can see, increased sugar levels not only lead to one system or organ being affected, and leading to only one disease process of diabetes to develop, but rather it leads to a whole range of organs, systems and disease processes to become involved.

The only way to effectively reverse type 2 diabetes (or even pre-diabetes) is to deal with the underlying cause of Insulin Resistance. Trying to address the blood sugar levels (with medication) without addressing the insulin levels is treating the symptoms, not treating the root cause. Just think of using a bucket to remove water from an overflowing sink rather than actually turning off the tap. The most important thing to do is to stop adding fuel to the fire. If Insulin Resistance is driving the condition, you need to first stop consuming foods that increase insulin production. See Chapter 8 where I discuss how to swap out these simple fuels for healthy, tasty complex fuels.

When you get to the cause of the issue instead of just treating the symptoms, you can actually change the environment that you are providing for your body, and normal function can be restored and healing can happen from within.

2-Inflammation

Did you know that all degenerative processes in the body are due to inflammation? Think about all of the conditions which end in "itis." "Itis" is the Greek suffix meaning inflammation, and is one of the building blocks used to construct medical terms. For example, colitis is literally colon inflammation or, figuratively, inflammation of the colon. Arthritis is inflammation of the arthros, or joints. Cellulitis is inflammation of the deeper layers of the skin, iritis is inflammation of the iris in your eye, appendicitis is inflammation of your appendix. You get the idea.

Everything in the body happens for a reason, and it is when the normal processes become chronically stimulated that signs and symptoms of disease show up. Inflammation also falls into this category.

Inflammation is a natural and very important defence mechanism in your body, and is directly tied to your immune system. One of the purposes of your immune system is to recognize damaged cells, irritants, and pathogens, and then begin to dispose of them in order to keep you healthy. Your immune system is your waste disposal system. It collects all of the trash and ushers it out of the body. This is definitely a good system to have in place, as you do not want to have these kinds of irritants floating around in your body.

Inflammation in your body occurs in response to an irritant within your body. It can be a physical or a chemical irritant. Stubbing your toe or spraining your ankle is a physical trauma or irritant, and your body will respond with swelling and inflammation to protect the injured tissues as they take time to heal and recover their normal function again.

When you have a sore throat due to an illness, your immune system will send in white blood cells, resulting in swelling and inflammation of your lymph nodes to trap and contain the irritant. During inflammation chemicals from the white blood cells are released into the blood, or the affected tissues, to protect your body from the foreign substances. This release of chemicals increases the blood flow to the area of injury or infection, and may result in redness and warmth. The increase in blood flow is a mechanism for flushing out the irritant from the site of injury or infection. However, as with every system in the body, if the system is chronically stimulated the end result is excessive wear and tear. Then the system begins to break down, and signs and symptoms of the degenerative disease process begin to show up.

When inflammation is chronically stimulated in the body, this can eventually cause the development of several conditions and diseases including some cancers and rheumatoid arthritis. On the one hand, it is your body's natural way of protecting itself when you are injured or sick, but when the system is working overtime it can actually make you sick.

Inflammatory diseases include a vast array of disorders and conditions. Examples include all allergies, as these are simply the body's overactive inflammatory response to a stimulus. Not everyone is allergic to grass, but if your body presents with an overactive response to grass you will experience watery eyes, sneezing, itching, and many other irritating symptoms when you are exposed to grass. Other examples of inflammatory diseases include asthma, autoimmune diseases, coeliac disease, glomerulonephritis, hepatitis, inflammatory bowel disease, and transplant rejection.

When inflammation is chronically sustained in your body, there is an increased risk of diseases like diabetes, heart disease, and obesity.

Interestingly, the foods you eat can have a major effect on inflammation in your body. Foods that cause inflammation, swelling of cell membranes, and therefore pain, include processed meats, sugary drinks, trans fats found in fried foods, white bread and pasta, gluten, soybean oil and vegetable oil. These are the "white" foods that I talk about. This encompasses wheat, dairy, sugar and gluten.

As you begin to swap out these bad fuels for your body I will now share here, as well as in Chapter 8, some anti-inflammatory foods which you can incorporate into your meals. Eating all of the colours of the rainbow is very important when decreasing inflammation in your body. Eat greens, reds, blues and purples, and not just fruits but your vegetables too. Tree nuts are also a great addition here, but not peanuts as they are not a true nut. Turmeric is an incredible anti-inflammatory with many other health benefits. It is a wonderful seasoning, and I encourage you to begin using it in your daily cooking.

As I have mentioned previously, it is not just all about food. Exercising, keeping stress levels at bay, and getting good sleep all have an impact on the inflammatory response in your body. This is why it is important to nourish all aspects of your mind, body and spirit naturally for enhanced vitality and optimal health.

3-Arthritis

Arthritis means joint inflammation, but did you know that the term is also used to describe 200 conditions which affect joints, the tissues that surround the joints, and other connective tissues as well? The most common form of arthritis is osteoarthritis, which affects millions of people worldwide. It occurs when the protective cartilage on the ends of your bones wears down over time. Osteoarthritis is simply another wear and tear degenerative process. Although osteoarthritis can result when any joint in your body is damaged, it most commonly affects joints in your hands, knees, hips and spine.

Other common rheumatic conditions related to arthritis include gout, fibromyalgia, and rheumatoid arthritis. Certain rheumatic conditions can also involve the immune system and various internal organs of the body.

Some forms of arthritis, such as rheumatoid arthritis and lupus (SLE), can affect multiple organs and cause widespread symptoms. Again, nothing happens in isolation in the body.

According to the Center for Disease Control and Prevention (CDC), 54.4 million adults in the United States have received a diagnosis of some form of arthritis. Of these, 23.7 million people have their activity curtailed in some way due to their condition. Arthritis is more common among adults aged 65 years or older, but it can affect people of all ages, including children. This is not only a painful condition, but it also adversely affects the quality of life for a large segment of the population. This also leads to increased health care costs.

There are many factors which contribute to the development of arthritis. When you have sustained an injury to any part of your skeleton, over the course of time the repair process that your body undergoes leads to the stabilization of the injured joint, but also leads to arthritic formations within that injured joint. Other factors that affect the development of arthritis are abnormal metabolism, genetic makeup, infections, and immune system dysfunction.

Osteoarthritis is often treated with pain-reducing medications, physical activity, and weight loss if the person is overweight. You may wonder why physical activity is used for treating osteoarthritis. Even though the joints may be worn, staying physically active helps to promote blood flow throughout the body, and this in turn helps to nourish the tissues with the building blocks they need to regenerate and repair. Physical activity also helps to maintain joint mobility and function, and prevent stiffening of the joints.

With arthritis and joint inflammation there are a number of key foods to avoid. Processed foods such as baked goods and pre-packaged meals and snacks contain trans fats to help preserve them. The problem is that the trans fats trigger systemic inflammation throughout your body. When reading labels you can identify trans fats as any food containing partially hydrogenated oils.

Foods that contain refined sugar, such as pastries, chocolate, candy, soda, and even fruit juices, will also trigger the release of proteins in the body called cytokines, which cause even more inflammation. Sugar is labeled many different ways on food items. Some common things to watch out for are corn syrup, fructose, sucrose, or maltose in the list of ingredients.

Red meat and fried foods should also be avoided as they are high in saturated fats. This will cause increased cholesterol levels, and lead to even more inflammation in the body. On top of this, meat also contains high levels of advanced glycation end products (AGEs) which also stimulate inflammation, particularly when meat is cooked by broiling, grilling, roasting, or frying. But it is not just fried chicken you should avoid. Other fried foods, such as donuts and french fries, also contain trans fats as well as AGEs.

Refined grains including white bread, white pasta, and crackers all cause a spike in blood glucose levels, which has been shown to increase levels of several inflammation-markers in the body. Another factor to consider about grains is the gluten. People with gluten sensitivities may experience increased joint pain and inflammation when consuming wheat products.

Dairy products including cheese and high-fat dairy items like butter, ice cream and cream cheese, along with margarine and mayonnaise, are all high in both saturated fats and AGEs. These are all big inflammation triggers and should be avoided when you want to reverse disease processes.

Corn, peanut, sunflower, safflower, and soy oils are all high in omega-6 fatty acids. These fatty acids are healthy in small doses, but excessive omega-6 consumption can trigger inflammatory chemicals in your body.

This is not the case for the types of oils rich in omega-3 fatty acids, such as olive and flaxseed oils. These sources of omega-3 fatty acids are healthy, even in larger amounts.

Avoiding foods and drinks that trigger inflammation is not just good for your arthritis. An anti-inflammatory diet can also help prevent other chronic conditions like heart disease and diabetes.

Along with making different food choices, physical activity also has a positive effect on arthritis, and can cause a decrease in pain by increasing healing as the delivery of oxygen and nutrients is increased to the tissues via the circulatory system. This leads to improved function and mobility as the joints and tissues begin to limber up, and improves your mental and emotional state as your mobility improves and you are able to enjoy your life again. This is a clear illustration of how nothing works in isolation in the body. Everything is connected.

4-Cardiovascular Disease

There are many components to cardiovascular disease. Just as the name implies, 'cardio' refers to the heart and 'vascular' relates to your circulatory system and all of the blood vessels. Now lets walk through the stages of progression of cardiovascular disease. Blood pressure issues are the first indicator of dysfunction and are a reflection of the state of health of your blood vessels. As blood pressure issues continue your heart then has to work harder in order to pump the blood throughout your body. Heart disease occurs when the heart has to work harder than normal and angina becomes evident when there has been damage to the heart muscle resulting in abnormal function. A heart attack is the loss of function of the heart muscle and all of these conditions have their origins in the state of health of the blood vessels.

Disease of the blood vessels does not just occur in one region of your body. Your blood travels throughout your entire body, and blood vessels supply oxygen and nutrients to every single cell of your body. If you have atherosclerosis (hardening of the arteries) then it will be present throughout the entire body.

As a side note, erectile dysfunction is the first clinical indicator of generalized cardiovascular disease because blood flows everywhere. This is the canary in the coal mine. It is the first sign of significant endothelial vascular disease much earlier than a heart attack would present. Your body is not compartmentalized, as blood is delivered everywhere in the body and if you have vascular disease anywhere then you have it everywhere.

For the most part, treatment of these conditions traditionally consists of medications. Why are chemicals being used to change your blood pressure falsely instead of changing how you use your body, by incorporating exercise and what you provide for your body in regards to nourishment, in order to allow it to function optimally?

Research has shown that prolonged stretching such as in the form of yoga, along with moderate aerobic exercise, like taking a daily 30 minute walk, along with providing better fuels for your body, will reduce cholesterol levels and significantly reverse hardening of the arteries in adults who were shown to have coronary atherosclerotic disease. This reversal occurred simply by them adding daily stretching to their routine. Changing the environment that you provide for you body does truly change your outcomes.

You can help reduce your risk of heart disease by avoiding fried fast food and processed foods containing vegetable shortening.

Here is a quick list of some of the best foods you can eat to free your arteries of build-up. A handful of healthy nuts such as almonds or walnuts will satisfy your hunger and help your heart. Dark berries such as blueberries, strawberries, cranberries or raspberries are packed with phytonutrients and soluble fibre. Flaxseeds contain omega-3 fatty acids, fibre and phytoestrogens and consuming them in ground or milled form will enable you to reap the greatest benefit. Steel cut wheat free oats are a fantastic alternative to typical breakfast cereals and are a healthy way to start your day. Dark beans such as kidney or black beans are high in fibre, B-vitamins, and minerals. Red, yellow and orange veggies such as carrots, sweet potatoes, red peppers and acorn squash are packed with carotenoids, fibre and vitamins to help your heart. Spinach is also important and is easy to use in sandwiches and salads instead of lettuce.

Fruits such as oranges, cantaloupes and papaya are rich in beta-carotene, potassium, magnesium and fibre. Asparagus is filled with nutrients such as beta-carotene, folate and fibre. Tomatoes provide lycopene, vitamin C and alpha- and beta-carotene. Dark chocolate is good for your heart health, but just be sure that it is at least 70 percent cocoa. Crisp, fresh broccoli florets dipped in hummus are also a terrific healthy snack with nutrients including vitamins C and E, potassium, folate, calcium and fibre.

Choosing a variety of healthy fats such as extra virgin olive oil, coconut oil, flax seed oil, avocado oil and foods containing natural fats like nuts, seeds, avocado, and olives is also recommended.

Olive oil intake has been shown to be associated with decreased risk of heart disease. It not only helps protect the heart but also helps protect the cells that line your blood vessels from being damaged by overly reactive oxygen molecules. The result is that the cellular walls of the blood vessels remain strong. It also decreases blood pressure and has a protective effect against cancers of the upper digestive system, of the breast and of the respiratory system.

You may be noticing a trend in the recommended foods which are helpful in reducing the signs of these degenerative diseases. I encourage you to take just a few of these recommendations and begin to incorporate them into your daily routine. It will not take long before you begin to notice changes in how your body is functioning.

5-Cancer

During the course of every single waking moment your body is aging and cellular breakdown is occurring. Not to worry as this is exactly what is supposed to happen. During the day just a few of the activities that your body is participating in are moving, eating, thinking, and metabolizing, along with many others. As this occurs, all of the cells in your body are little powerhouses which create energy. With energy production also comes the creation of waste products. These wastes need to be excreted from your body. Throughout all of this there is also cell wear and tear, cell turnover and cell death. Cell turnover occurs mostly during your periods of sleep as many of the functions of the body are also at rest and this is when cellular repair and cellular regeneration occurs. All of the trillions of cells in your body have a limited life span and new cells are created to replace them as they die off. Your cells are grouped together in very specific and precise ways in order to form tissues and organs such as muscles, bones, the lungs and the liver. There are genes inside every single cell to tell it when to grow, work, divide and die. Normally, cells follow these instructions and the body remains healthy. At times the instructions get mixed up, causing cells to grow and divide out of control or to not die when they should. As more and more of these abnormal cells grow and divide, they can form a lump in the body called a tumour. Cancer, with its abnormal cell growth, also has the potential to invade or spread to other parts of the body. This happens when cancer cells get into the blood or lymphatic system. Even when a cancerous tumour is removed, cancerous tumours can reappear because cancer cells might have already spread from the tumour to other parts of the body.

It is important to detect cancer as early as possible, when it is usually smaller and easier to treat and there is less chance that the cancer has spread.

When cellular replication occurs at this accelerated rate during tumour growth, it requires a lot of energy in order to feed all of the new cells and this is why unexplained weight loss is often one of the first signs to present.

The genetic code for normal cellular function at times can undergo a mutation and this results in abnormal cellular behaviour. Most gene mutations occur after you are born and therefore are not inherited. A number of factors can cause mutations in the cellular genetic code and many of them are lifestyle related. Known causes of gene mutation include smoking, radiation of all sorts including ultrasound, x-ray and cellphones, viruses, cancer-causing chemicals known as carcinogens which are found in the environment and even in your food, obesity, hormones, as well as a lack of exercise.

Chronic inflammation may be caused by infections that don't go away, by an abnormal immune reaction to normal tissues, or by conditions such as obesity. Over time, chronic inflammation can cause genetic mutations and also lead to cancer.

Cancer is a serious health concern and it takes a toll mentally, emotionally, financially, spiritually, and physically on every person who is affected, not just the person who has been diagnosed with the disease. It causes stress in the mind and body of the patient as well as in their relationships with friends and family. Cancer treatments can make it hard to do the things that they had taken for granted and there is nothing in the daily existence of the patient that cancer does not touch.

There is good news! Experts estimate that more than half of the cases of cancer are preventable with lifestyle changes. The top 5 most-diagnosed cancers in men are lung, prostate, colon/colorectal, stomach, and liver. For women they are breast, colon/colorectal, lung, cervix, and stomach.

I point this out because you can see that several of the most common and the most aggressive cancers have to do with the gastrointestinal system. This system has as its main function to process the food you eat, distribute it around your body as needed, and does its best to dump the leftover toxins out of your body and it is exactly the system that is affected by cancer to the greatest degree! This is fantastic news because this is a major area of your daily life which you have control over and which you can also dramatically affect your outcomes.

The food and beverages you consume is the fuel your body uses to fight disease and is critical to your overall wellbeing. Some foods are worse for you than others and are increasing your risk of many conditions and diseases, not just cancer, as I have discussed heart disease, diabetes, obesity, and chronic inflammation in this chapter.

By reducing or eliminating these top 10 cancer causing foods you may be able to cut your cancer risk in half. Foods to avoid include the following: Genetically modified foods (GMO's) especially corn and soy; microwave popcorn as the chemically-lined bag as well as the actual contents is at the centre of lung cancer debates around the world; canned goods as most cans are lined with a product called bisphenol-A

(BPA); grilled red meat, as grilling changes the chemical and molecular structure of the meat; refined sugar and high-fructose corn syrup (HFCS) as this is the greatest cancer causing food by far; salted, pickled, and smoked foods typically contain preservatives, such as nitrates. (Please note that by pickled foods I am not referring to the fermented foods you make at home); soda and carbonated beverages filled with high-fructose corn syrup (HFCS), dyes, and a host of other chemicals are very bad for every aspect of your health. Adding "diet" to the label means you are also likely consuming aspartame which is no better than rat poison for your cells; white flour leads to increased insulin resistance and simple sugars like refined carbohydrates are the preferred fuel source for all cancer cells and therefore feeds cancer growth; farmed fish as they do not have as much omega-3 as wild; and hydrogenated vegetable oils have been proven to alter the structure of cell membranes in the body.

In addition to the 10 foods listed above, also be sure to avoid any food labeled as "diet," "light," or "fat-free." In order to remove fat or natural calories, they are then replaced with sugar and chemicals that are dangerous to your body. Instead of consuming food products that manufacturers claim are "good for you" I suggest that you follow these tips to prevent cancer the easy and natural way. Eat organic whenever possible. Choose raw or clean frozen if availability of fresh produce is not good in your area. Fill half your plate each meal with non-starchy vegetables. If you eat animal products, make sure they are grass-fed and free range meats. Use only high quality oils such as coconut oil, olive oil, and flax seed oil and cut back drastically on grains and sugars.

Not only will eliminating these foods lower your cancer risk but you are also going to feel and look better from the inside out. The long term effects of fuelling your body poorly can be seen when examining the state of the healthcare system. The effect is reaching in the trillions of dollars. There are increased office visits for ill health conditions, prescribed medications, costly investigations, ultrasound examinations, MRI and CT scans, invasive procedures and hospital stays. When you fuel your body well your cost to the healthcare system is very low and prevention is the key. As you change the environment that you are providing for your body you can change your health outcomes as well as reverse, reduce and prevent degenerative disease processes from occurring.

With this understanding of how truly remarkable your body is and that healing can happen, join me in the next chapter where I show you how to swap out the simple fuels which create so much inflammation and degeneration in your body, for delicious complex fuels that will create an environment in your body where you can heal your health.

When, If Not Now?

Record Your W.I.N.N.s Here

_____

_____

_____

_____

_____

_____

_____

_____

_____

_____

_____

_____

_____

_____

_____

_____

_____

_____

_____

_____

_____

_____

_____

_____

_____

Chapter 8

What Not To Eat

Conventional wisdom states that in order to get healthier you need to lose weight. The opposite is actually true. As you begin to gain your health, your body will begin to function better, metabolization will be improved, and you will begin to lose weight. Weight loss is a side benefit to getting healthy.
— Dr. Stacey Cooper

It is very difficult to trick the system; therefore, it is not your fault if you feel like you were not successful with your previous weight loss journeys. As I shared with you in Chapter 4, diets do not work. I have found that swapping out bad fuels for good, while still being able to enjoy your favourites, has been the key to the success of my clients, and will be for you too.

I know that you want to be healthy because you are already taking steps to ensure this. I know you want to be healthy because you are here with me right now. I also know that in this information age it is so very confusing to know what steps to take, and this is why I focus first on teaching the inner workings of the body. When you know *why* your body functions the way it does, it is much easier to follow through with the *how* to be successful with optimizing your health.

When you consider our historical origin of hunters and gatherers, and the scientific facts that your body comes out of the womb with all of the enzymes, hormones, neurological transmitters, and the biochemistry to sustain you for a lifetime, then it becomes an easy conclusion that the body requires and is capable of digesting foods of the earth only. I know that this can lead to some confusion because of all of the media hype and advertising noise. Did you know that even Canada's Food Guide and most public health food pyramids are forms of advertising? Dr. Yoni Freedhoff, medical director of the for-profit Bariatric Medical Institute and one of only three Canadian physicians certified as an obesity specialist states: "We don't have a food guide that reflects our current understanding on the impact of diet on disease, and that seems backwards in a country where diet and weight-related illnesses are the number one preventable causes of death." His full report can be found at http://thetyee.ca/News/2014/10/20/Canada-Food-Guide/.[2]

I am sharing with you how to partner your food choices with nutrition, so that you can experience how wellness isn't difficult. It just gets easier and easier, and it is more and more rewarding as you begin to notice improvements in how you feel and how your body is functioning. Food choices can be so overwhelming. So many choices, so many conveniences, so many theories, and no idea which road to take. I will discuss not only what foods to avoid but I will also share with you easy options to swap out the bad fuels for great, healthy, nutritious and delicious alternatives in order to fuel your engine for optimal performance. One of the key reasons why this works is because you can still have your favourites; you will just create them a little differently.

As I have shared with you, it is my recommendation that you do not eat any food stuffs that are white. White is not a colour of the rainbow, and any food that is white should be avoided. This includes wheat, all dairy products and sugar.

[2] The newest version of Canada's Food Guide was released on January 21, 2019, and is a vast improvement over the 12 year old version Dr. Freedhoff was referring to. Health Canada states that the food industry was not involved in the creation of the new version. The new guide recommends water as the drink of choice, and places greater emphasis on a plant-based diet, and I am in full agreement with this.

1-Wheat

The wheat of today is not what it used to be. It has been genetically modified and grows differently. The manufacturing process also strips the wheat of any of its nutritional value as it is first milled, then highly refined and bleached into white flour.

We have previously talked about simple fuels, and how they are detrimental because they lead to spikes in blood sugar levels. Wheat does exactly the same thing. When it is ingested it is immediately absorbed and stresses the pancreas, and then insulin levels rise. This is the diabetic connection (see Chapters 6 and 7).

As I discussed in Chapter 7, wheat increases blood sugar greater than white table sugar, as evident when utilizing the glycemic index.

The Glycemic Index, (GI) is the measure of how much blood sugar levels increase in the 90-120 minutes after a food is consumed. By this measure, whole wheat bread has a GI of 72, while plain table sugar has a GI of only 59. In contrast, kidney beans have a GI of 51, a grapefruit is at 25, while non-carbohydrate foods such as salmon and walnuts have GIs of essentially zero, which means that eating these particular foods has no effect on blood sugar levels. Foods that can spike blood sugar like wheat are very few but do include dried sugar-rich fruits like dried dates and figs. They are dehydrated so the sugar is much more concentrated and more accessible therefore they raise blood sugar levels.

It is also very interesting that pulverized starches such as cornstarch, rice starch, potato starch, and tapioca starch all have high glycemic indexes. It is worth noting that these are the very same carbohydrates often used to make gluten-free food.

Food manufacturers have tried to fill the niche of providing gluten-free products to those who are sensitive to, or who choose to eliminate, gluten from their diets. The problem is that they use cornstarch, rice starch, potato starch and tapioca starch to make these gluten-free foods. The result is a product that is still not good for you! In November 2013, Dr. William Davis, author of the "Wheat Belly" book, spoke at the Sanderson Centre in Brantford, Ontario. When he was asked about wheat elimination and substituting gluten-free foods, this was his response: "Think of wheat as a cigarette. We all know that cigarettes are bad for your health. Now we know that wheat is bad for us so think of wheat as a cigarette. Well now you can view gluten-free foods as being like a cigarette with a filter. It is still not good for you. It is still a cigarette!" The reason behind this is that gluten-free products are made by replacing wheat with cornstarch, rice starch, potato starch, or tapioca starch. These are all simple fuels and lead to the same spike in blood sugar levels as wheat does. They have the same diabetic connection, and are therefore still detrimental to your system. They also lead to the deposition of visceral "wheat belly" fat which prevents you from losing weight.

Another issue with wheat is gluten. Gluten is the protein in the wheat. When you ingest this, it coats the intestines with the glue, and leads to a reduction in the absorption of the rest of the nutritious food you are providing for your body. The result can be malabsorption issues, as well as inflammation of the digestive tract.

Other grains that contain gluten include barley, rye, spelt, triticale, kamut and oats. In order to eliminate gluten you must also eliminate these grains. As a side note, oats which are labeled steel-cut and wheat-free are acceptable to include in your diet.

When looking to swap out your wheat products there are many easy alternatives. When considering wheat products, your list may include things like bread, muffins, cookies, cakes, pasta, pizza, as well as others. You may have believed that you had this covered by using gluten-free foods. These are not a great swap for wheat products. Remember that I told you that you can still have your favourites, and that you can just make them a little differently. Here is how! Using almond meal for chocolate chip cookies as well as for marvelous muffins is a great start. Swapping out wheat flour when baking breakfast breads and my baba's banana bread recipe with brown rice flour, coconut flour and amaranth flour enables our kids to enjoy this long-standing family tradition. It is also very easy to enjoy apple cake and luscious chocolate cake too, and it only takes 7 minutes to make. All of these easy recipes are included in my Healthy Fuels Cookbook™.

Elimination of wheat can yield rapid weight loss due to the combination of halting the glucose-insulin-fat-deposition cycle and the natural reduction in cravings, which leads to a reduced calorie intake.

As I was coaching a couple through my lecture series, the husband was in the office for his chiropractic adjustment. I asked how his day was going, as he had just started being wheat-free. He replied, "Great!" He reported that they had a vegan, dairy-free smoothie for breakfast, he had packed a salad with nuts and seeds for his lunch, and was drinking his 2 litres of water. I then asked what was planned for supper. He said they were going to have homemade burgers. I said "FANTASTIC! Now just get rid of the bun and you will have accomplished a whole day of wheat-free!!" There are so many alternatives that enable you to still be able to enjoy your favourites; you just have to think outside the box. To replace a bun, use romaine lettuce leaves, or even a red pepper sliced in half and flattened a little. You can also use thinly sliced eggplant that has been grilled. Another delicious alternative is to grill 2 portobello mushrooms for your burger bun. The options are endless, and it is fun to be creative.

2-Dairy Products

As discussed in Chapter 6, calcium from dairy products is not the most absorbable form and therefore your body cannot utilize it. Remember that when I talk about dairy products this not only includes cow's milk, but all dairy products created from all sources of mammals' milk, including butter, yogurt, cheese, cottage cheese, cream cheese, cheese dips, ice cream, frozen desserts, sherbets, sorbets, frozen yogurt, whey protein and milk powder.

All whole foods contain the essential nutrient calcium, not just dairy products as we have been led to believe through advertising and the media. The calcium in dairy products is not absorbable by the body, as magnesium is not present in the milk. Magnesium is necessary to activate Vitamin D, the carrier that calcium requires in order for it to be taken up by the cells of the body, so that the body can utilize it. When you consume your nutrients from whole food sources, your body receives all the nutrients it requires, and uptake of nutrients into cells occurs normally and the body thrives.

As mentioned earlier, some foods leave an acidic residue once metabolized, and some leave an alkaline residue. Dairy products leave an acidic residue in the body. In order for the body to balance the resulting rise in blood acidity, it will take calcium from the bones to buffer the blood. This leads to weakening of the bones, and the result is osteoporosis. The higher the rate of dairy consumption, the higher the risk of hip fractures, which is a prime indicator of osteoporosis. North America has the highest consumption of dairy products and the highest incidence of osteoporosis.

Milk and other dairy products are the top source of saturated fat in the North American diet, contributing to heart disease, type 2 diabetes, and Alzheimer's disease. Studies have also linked dairy to an increased risk of breast, ovarian, and prostate cancers.

So why is it that we consume dairy products? What good does it do for our bodies?

If you need a "milk" source then I can suggest some great sources. Almond milk, coconut milk, and cashew milk are all pressed nut milks, are a great source of protein, and are great in smoothies. They are also very easy to make at home. Just remember that it is not cow's milk, so it will not taste the same. The best thing to drink is water. Whether you infuse it with some fruit or lemon slices, or anything natural, water is all that your body needs.

Some great fuels for the body and alternative sources of calcium include the following. Seeds such as pumpkin, sesame, sunflower and cotton are tiny nutritional powerhouses. They are delicious on their own, add great texture to any salads, muffins and stir frys. They also make wonderful seed butters, that you can use everywhere you would use peanut butter.

When consuming nuts and seeds, which are a great source of many nutrients as well as healthy fats, I never recommend peanuts or peanut butter as they are not a true nut, and they actually have many health conditions associated with their consumption. If you would like more information about peanuts email me at drstacey@drstacey cooper.com with subject: Peanuts.

Lentils, beans such as kidney, white, mung, cow, lima, and chickpeas, along with almonds, leafy green vegetables, the grain amaranth, and figs, are also great sources of calcium.

When looking to swap out your dairy products there are many easy alternatives. Avocados are an excellent source of many nutrients, as well as a great source of healthy fats and fibre. You can use them to create creamy dips and dressings, as well as puddings and mayonnaise. Nutritional yeast is an excellent replacement for cheese. I use it for making cheese sauces for lasagna, and creating vegan parmesan cheese. Full fat coconut milk replaces whipping cream and cream for soups, sauces and dips, and I use it in baking and cooking, anywhere that would call for dairy milk. I also have recipes for soups, sour cream, cheesecake, chocolate ice cream, pudding and mousse. Alternatives are easy when you have the tools at your fingertips.

3-Simple Sugars

Simple sugars include refined white table sugar. The more processing that any food source undergoes, the lower the nutritional content becomes. As sugar becomes more refined, it is broken down into smaller and smaller particles. It is stripped of any fibre, healthful minerals or other nutrients. The end result is simple glucose molecules that immediately enter the blood stream. This is how it can easily dissolve when stirred into liquids. The same occurs when you ingest it. It is easily metabolized, rapidly released into the blood stream, and causes a severe spike in blood sugar levels. As this happens, the pancreas begins to produce even more insulin. This is Type 2 Diabetes. So if you change the fuel you provide for your body, you can break this cycle and this won't happen.

Here I will share with you how to swap out simple white table sugar for complex sugars which take longer for your system to break down, therefore eliminating the diabetic connection.

Not all sugars are created equal. Some are absorbed more readily than others. Some sugars are more complex, and therefore take longer for your system to break them down and to digest. This results in a more gradual release of the molecules into your blood stream. These complex sugars will not dissolve as easily in the stomach, the digestive enzymes will take longer to break them down, and there will be a much more gradual release into the blood stream. These complex sugars need to be digested and metabolized first, which is the natural process. Only after this metabolization are the resultant simple glucose molecules gradually released into the blood stream, at a slower rate. This enables the pancreas to continue to hum along steadily, and the insulin can manage the sugar load. This eliminates the spiking of the blood sugar levels, and the precursor of diabetes. This is how improved normal body function occurs when providing complex fuels for your body. This is much easier for your insulin levels to deal with, and reduces the stress on your pancreas. The right sources of fuel for your body are important for keeping energy production at optimal levels.

Consumption of simple sugars leads to an elevation in levels of bad cholesterol, an increase in inflammation throughout the body, an increase in heart disease, and an increase in obesity.

The good news is that this metabolic syndrome can be reversed by providing low-insulin-potential foods for your system. This helps you decrease the load on your pancreas. You will then make less insulin and it will allow you to use it more effectively. You will know you are experiencing success when your cravings diminish and then disappear completely. This is when your healing will begin.

The right source of sugars are unrefined natural sugars. I promised you that I am not going to eliminate anything; you can still have your sugar, although greatly decreasing your sugar intake is a fantastic idea, I am changing the fuel that you are providing for your body so that you can experience better body function. Examples of these include, but are not limited to, the following natural complex sugars.

Pure honey has many healthful benefits. As I was researching things I came across information that said that if you are to be a true vegan, you cannot consume honey as it is an animal product. If you choose to eat honey, it is my recommendation to be sure to get unpasteurized honey because, as with any food processing, pasteurization kills all of the healthful benefits. Honey has many healthy benefits. It is a natural antibiotic as well as a complex natural sugar. It is sweeter that brown rice syrup, so be sure to take this into account when substituting it in recipes.

Another complex sugar which is very easy to use is organic brown rice syrup. It is an excellent sweetener for baking, and can easily replace corn syrup in your recipes as it is not as sweet as honey. This is what is in the energy packed and nutritious sunflower bars found in my recipe book.

100% pure maple syrup is a complex sugar and has a wonderful flavour. I am not talking about the grocery store pancake syrup because the first ingredient in this is high fructose corn syrup. This is a simple sugar, and spikes blood sugar levels as well as increases cravings. 100% pure maple syrup is very versatile and easy to use.

Pitted dates are a great source of fibre and an easy sweetener for anything blended, like smoothies, baked good, or chocolate pudding.

Another easy swap is organic coconut sugar. It is unrefined and is a complex fuel. It is suitable to replace white or brown sugars in all of your recipes with a 1:1 ratio.

I also recommend that as you are shifting how you are fuelling your body, begin to cut down the sugar that you add to foods. Your body will adapt to every environment that you provide. As you begin to cut down the amount of sugar you use, your tastebuds will change and you will find that you begin to prefer less sugar. This is another win! You will also then experience the natural sugars that are present in whole foods, allowing the natural sugars to tickle your taste buds.

Do you see how this is doable? By making these changes you are not depriving yourself of anything. You will just be replacing them with different choices, thereby providing what I call "high octane fuels" for your engine so that optimal function can be achieved.

4-Bad Fats

As with everything else, not all fats are created equal. Some are more readily digested and absorbed than others. These include natural unprocessed fats. Some fats clog up your system and are not able to be metabolized, and are left to be stored in your body as toxins. The right sources of good fats for your body are important in order to keep energy production and your overall health at optimal levels.

When choosing healthy fats, things to look for include sources of omega-3 (alpha-linolenic acid), omega-6 (linoleic acid) essential fatty acids, omega-9 (oleic acids) non-essential fatty acids as well as polyunsaturated fats and mono-unsaturated fats. 20% to 30% of your daily intake of calories should come from good fats. Your choices of fat can have a huge effect on your overall health, as good fats will raise your level of good cholesterol and lower your levels of bad cholesterol as well as reduce inflammation, lower blood pressure, and control blood clotting. The omega-3s have anti-inflammatory benefits and help prevent heart disease and joint pain. Omega-6s lower blood cholesterol and support the skin, while omega-9s help to lower LDL ("bad") cholesterol and raise HDL ("good") cholesterol as well as help to control blood sugar levels. Like all fats, these fatty acids also provide energy for your body.

Bad fats will raise your risk of type II diabetes and heart disease. The wrong sources of fats include all fats and oils that are not in their natural state. When processing, additives, preservatives, colouring and chemicals are added. These are not normally occurring substances, and your body does not recognize them. Your body only has digestive enzymes to process foods of the earth. All of the unrecognized additives are then shuttled off to the filtering organs of the body, the liver and kidneys, and are then stored in your fat tissue. This is how your body becomes fat and toxic.

As you can see, healthy fats play a very important role in optimizing many functions of your body. I encourage you to read on as I will discuss easy to find sources of healthy fats for your body, and easy ways to implement them into your daily life.

Udo's Oil contains the omega 3, 6 and 9 essential fatty acids. Often our diets lack natural good sources of these fatty acids; therefore I do encourage a well-sourced product like Udo's Oil.

Cod liver oil is another amazing fat source, and contains docosahexaenoic acid (DHA). The Nordic Naturals citrus flavoured arctic cod liver oil is excellent for putting into smoothies, as you will never even know it is in there.

DHA is a structural fat, making up approximately 30% of the structural fats in the grey matter of the brain and 97% of the omega-3's in the brain. Studies have shown that DHA plays a role in infant mental development, brain and nervous system development and function, as well as neurological health. This means that any disease process which affects the nervous system, such as Alzheimer's, Parkinson's, and Multiple Sclerosis, may be combated by consuming DHA and healthful fats.

Flaxseed and flaxseed oil contain alpha-linolenic acid (ALA), which helps your body to utilize the essential omega-3 fatty acids in your body. There is evidence that flaxseed and flaxseed oil may lower levels of bad cholesterol. Ground flax seeds are also helpful with menopausal symptoms. It is similar to hormone therapy without the drugs. Research has shown that 40 grams of ground flaxseeds per day may be similar to hormone therapy for improving mild menopause symptoms, such as hot flashes and night sweats. Ground flaxseed may also ease constipation as it is a great source of insoluble fibre. Flaxseed oil is great for making salad dressings and glazes.

Another great fat is cold pressed olive oil. It is a very healthy oil and tastes great, but it does not tolerate heat very well. I do not recommend that you use this for cooking. When you cook with olive oil, it will smoke. This is due to the denaturing of the oil. Just like high heat processing during food manufacturing, the heating of the olive oil results in you losing the healthful benefits.

Olive oil intake is associated with decreased risk of heart disease. It not only helps protect the heart, but also helps protect the cells that line our blood vessels from being damaged by overly reactive oxygen molecules. The result is that the cellular walls of the blood vessels remain strong. It also decreases blood pressure and has a protective effect against cancers of the upper digestive system, breast, and respiratory system.

A great oil to use for cooking and sautéeing is coconut oil, as it handles higher heats very well. This is what you can replace your butter with when cooking. Of course an unrefined source is best, and it will be solid at room temperature. If it is liquid at room temperature, it has been refined and processed.

Coconut oil, when digested and broken down, forms a mono-glyceride called monolaurin. This can kill harmful pathogens such as bacteria, viruses and fungi such as the bacteria Staphylococcus Aureus (a very dangerous pathogen) as well as Candida Albicans, the source of yeast infections. Coconut oil also improves levels of good and bad cholesterol, leads to a reduced risk of heart disease, and also to immediate improvement in brain function in patients with mild forms of Alzheimer's.

More great sources of good fats include avocados, nuts and seeds. They are delicious and so versatile. Because of their healthy fat and fibre content, they do a great job at satisfying your satiation centre in the brain, and this enables you to consume less calories.

Not all fats are created equal. Fats to avoid include trans fats, hydrogenated fats, lard, vegetable shortening, processed vegetable oils, and margarine. Every one of these types of fat have been manufactured; they are not naturally occurring. They are not a good source for your body.

5-Anything Artificial, Packaged Or Processed

By this point you and I have taken quite a journey, and I have shared a lot with you about how your body was designed and what fuels it can utilize well.

The title of this book does wrap it all up in a nutshell, "Heal Your Health — Nourishing Your Mind, Body and Spirit Naturally." From this alone you may deduce that only things which are found in nature should be consumed, and to this I say YES! Now let's delve into why food "stuffs" that are artificial, packaged or processed should be avoided.

Anything that is artificial by definition did not come from the earth, and therefore cannot be digested by your enzymes. Your body only has enzymes for digesting foods of the earth. Artificial substances have been created in a laboratory and are made up of chemicals.

Anything that you cannot pronounce or cannot understand does not belong in your body. Chemicals and preservatives are created for the sole purpose of prolonging shelf life. What do you think your body would do with such "ingredients?" Nothing! The body cannot metabolize chemicals; it can't excrete them, it can't void them, it can only store them. The body cannot digest them so they get locked into the liver, kidneys and adipose/fat tissue, and this is how your body becomes toxic.

Take a moment now and imagine the inside of your grocery store. When you buy a cucumber, does it have a label? Does it have an ingredient list? No! It is a cucumber. You know it is a cucumber just by looking at it. It is not manufactured; it is a whole food. Whole foods are how I choose to fuel my body.

Getting rid of everything artificial includes colouring, flavouring, and preservatives. Flavouring especially will have chemicals and toxins like aspartame, sucralose and fructose. This is a super concentrated sweetener which provides your body with extra calories and also stimulates your brain to demand more. As I shared with you in Chapter 4, in regards to the satiation centre feedback loop, it tricks the brain in regard to the richness of food and caloric content, and this is what leads you to have cravings.

The purpose of the processing of whole foods is to cut down preparation time. Because the "food" is processed, it is already partly broken down and may even be partially 'cooked' as well. This means that the food stuff is taken further and further away from its natural state, and there is less nutrient value remaining. All of the vitamins and minerals are stripped away during this process, so there is very little of the essential nutrients left for your body to use as building blocks for healthy cells and tissues. Processing is what enables a longer shelf life because there are very little organic nutrients left to rot.

As you begin to eliminate these chemicals and artificial products, you will want to be on the lookout for everything boxed, canned and packaged. Perhaps you can think of a few things that come in boxes and cans that you know you will already want to do without.

Added salt is the main preservative in canned products, as well as chemicals, in order to increase shelf life. When it comes to fruits and vegetables, fresh is best, but only if in season. The sun is our natural power source, and plants utilize the energy of the sun to create their fruit. In order for the fruit or vegetable to be packed full of all of the vitamins, minerals and nutrients that it was designed to have, it must be attached to the plant during the full course of ripening. If you are buying fresh but it is coming from another country or continent, it was not ripe when it was picked. If it had been ripe at the time of picking but then had to travel for days in order to reach your table, it would be spoiled by time it got to you. It did not ripen on the vine. It has ripened artificially while in transit. It would actually be better to purchase frozen if it is not available locally in season, because fruits and vegetables are flash frozen at the time of picking and the majority of nutrients remain intact.

As for boxed products, most are made with wheat, sugar, chemicals, additives, preservative, colourings etc. And now you know how detrimental these things are for your body. When you are ready to remove these items from your lifestyle, as with most things, you can go about this in two different ways. You can either grab a garbage bag and go cold turkey and remove all of these items from your house, or you can gradually wean off of them. To do this gradually I recommend that you just do not purchase any more of them. Once you use up what is at home just do not replace them. You will have to decide which will work best for you.

Now you are aware of what type of diet would best naturally support the function of your body in regards to the required nutrients essential for optimal body function, and that it would be best if they are acquired in their natural state. This is what will allow you to nourish your body to health. This is what will keep you healthy and allow you to enjoy enhanced vitality.

Do you recall that I shared with you the concept of good calories and bad calories? So make your calories count and you will not have to count your calories. Nourish your body well and you won't need to worry about calories. It will be your appetite that will let you know when you are full and satisfied.

Provide for your body a variety of complex fuels from a variety of sources, including all the colours of the rainbow, in order to ensure balanced nutrition and optimal functioning of your body, as well as enhanced vitality.

All of the information that I share with you here is not just something that I stumbled upon, or thought it would be fun to look up, or was just something to do to fill my time. Like I needed any more of my time occupied! This was born out of necessity, due to my own personal experience. In the next chapter I share with you my story.

When, If Not Now?

Record Your W.I.N.N.s Here

Chapter 9

Second Chances - My Story of Discovering Self-Love

The two most important days in your life are the day you are born...and the day you find out why.
— Mark Twain

Our little family had enjoyed a wonderful afternoon on that gorgeous day. Derek was just five months old, Kayla was two, and Lyndsay was four. We had just moved into our new country home in May. The kids had settled early in bed that night. Life was extremely hectic, and my husband Dean, my high school sweetheart, and I just wanted to take a breather. I just wanted my Calgon moment.

We had a new home, I had my chiropractic practice, and Dean was working shifts at the car manufacturing plant. We had a new hot tub, and we were going to take some much needed time for ourselves. What happened next was beyond anything that I ever contemplated. It was my wake-up call.

We were enjoying the sunshine, the breeze, and the warmth of the water. This was our little piece of heaven. Then...everything changed in an instant.

As we were relaxing in the hot tub I started to feel heavy pressure in my chest. I was experiencing heart palpitations, and I could not catch my breath. It was not long before total fear took over, and I was completely panic-stricken. Without Dean by my side, I would not have made it out of the tub. As it turns out, I was in the early stages of a heart attack. Of course, that was the furthest thing from my mind, as I was a healthy, vibrant, productive, thirty-three-year-old woman, with a young family, a new baby, and so many people depending on me. There was no way this could be happening to me. But it was.

We have been taught that we need to be Superwoman and that we have to do it all, or else we are considered weak. I am here to share with you a better way, that I learned from this experience. This is why self-love is of the utmost and greatest importance, and is my highest priority now. Without self-love there is no health, vibrancy, love of life, or existence for me.

I welcome you to join me on my journey.

Saturday, May 11th, 1996-Graduation Day

I graduated as a 4th generation doctor of chiropractic, from the same school as my dad and grandad. My great-grandfather started our practice in 1912 in our hometown of Brantford, Ontario. This was truly an incredible day for the entire family. Dean and I had been married for four years and he, along with both of our families, had supported me during my four years of university, and for the gruelling and intensive four years of chiropractic study. We were all very relieved, excited and emotional as my whole future opened up on that day.

Graduation was held at the University of Toronto, and we celebrated at the Royal York Hotel with our entire family. It was a day of pride, joy, accomplishment, and excitement, and it truly touched my heart as my dad and my father-in-law stood up and gave their speeches, congratulating us. My dad was bursting with pride, and my father-in-law was thrilled to be able to welcome a doctor into the Latimer family. I was deeply touched when Dean stood up to share his congratulations, and how proud he was of me and all that I had accomplished with all my hard work. He also then congratulated the new grandparents at the table. Yes, we were expecting our first baby! This was met with great whooping and hollering, tears of joy, lots of kisses around the table, as well as the lighting of cigars, I might add.

Life continued to unfold very happily for us. Dean was working full-time, and I started practicing with my dad. Two months later Lyndsay was born, and two years later Kayla arrived. I was balancing my practice and my home life, as I was in the office three days a week after an eight-week maternity leave with each of the girls. Being self-employed, if you're not in the office, you aren't getting paid, but the bills still come. My practice continued to grow, and Dad and I were working very well together.

Saturday, November 18th, 2000 -Everything Changes

That was the day that everything changed, the day Dad was no longer able to practice.

Four years prior, Dad was diagnosed with chronic inflammatory demyelinating polyneuropathy. It is an auto-immune condition and had been managed, but on this day, he was no longer physically able to work. I was four months pregnant with our third child.

At that moment I had no concerns at all because of course I was *expected* to handle it all. My life was turned completely upside down, and I do not ever remember a time when I felt such overwhelm. I had to interview and hire babysitters and then schedule care for the girls around Dean's shifts. The stress I experienced was incredible, as I was managing the full caseload of two practices as well as running our business entirely on my own. We did not know if Dad would be able to come back to the office or not. There was always hope, but in the end, he never did return.

The month prior a very dear high school friend of ours had lost her husband due to an adverse medical reaction. She then found herself living in her childhood country home with her two young children, all alone. At Christmas time she decided to move to the city, closer to her parents. She was thrilled to give us the opportunity to have a country property which we had always dreamed of. My dad's advice at this time was, "If this is where you want to be and what you want to do, don't let money stand in your way!" We were to become new homeowners.

February 2001-No Time for Relaxin'

As much as I love practicing chiropractic, it was taking its toll on my body physically. Along with working full-time, we were also in the process of selling our home and packing up to move. I was very pregnant, and I was in the office adjusting patients forty hours per week. We practice full-spine manual adjusting, so my work is very physical. At this point, I had to wear a support belt to hold my pelvis and sacroiliac joints together. When the end of the pregnancy draws near, the body prepares by secreting the hormone relaxin. This enables ligaments to loosen and to allow the pelvis to open and become more flexible in preparation for the passage of the baby during delivery. I was working a lot. Too much. I was thoroughly enjoying each moment at the office, but it was all I could do, at the end of the long days, to crawl into an Epsom salt bath to relieve my aching, tired muscles, then straight to bed in order to do it all over again the next day. I was missing my girls, my husband, and my dad. At that point, it was business as usual. There was no time to feel anything; the tasks at hand were too great to leave any room for feelings.

My due date was March 30th.

For my other two pregnancies, it was always Dad who took care of my patients while I was on my eight-week maternity leave. I did not have that option this time around, so I had to go through the process of hiring a locum who would be suitable to take care of our patients. We originally decided to have him enter the practice on March 15th, but we had him come into the office on Monday, March 5th instead. This turned out to be a very good idea.

Friday, March 9, 2001-Derek Arrives

Friday, March 9th started out just like so many other Fridays before, where I would drop the girls at the sitter's at 8 am. On this Friday Dean was working nights. He would pick the girls up at lunchtime, and they would all nap at home together. I was then expected to arrive home just after 4 pm. Dean would have supper ready, and then he would head off to work twenty minutes after I walked in the door. That was the game plan.

This is what actually happened:

I dropped Lyndsay and Kayla off at 8 am as planned. As I was leaning over two-year-old Kayla to unzip her coat, I felt a stitch. This was three weeks prior to my due date, so I didn't think anything of it. On hindsight, that was the start of my labour.

I went to the office and continued to prepare the locum to take over our practice, and I continued to do the majority of the adjusting too. Occasionally, I would have to pause and stop to allow tension in my abdomen to pass. At noon I checked in with my midwife. She determined that what I called 'abdominal tension' was labour contractions which were one minute long! She then said, "You get yourself home, put your feet up and then we can determine whether this is false labour or not." Well, that was put on hold as Dad dropped into the office. He wanted to check on things and see how the locum was doing.

As I was giving Dad his adjustment, he asked how my day was going. That is when I said, "Well, I've been in labour all day." He just about freaked! He told me to alert Mom and to get myself home. I had not yet spoken with Dean. Boy, was he going to get a surprise when I got home! I sorted everything with the locum, and I was able to leave the office at 3:10 pm. As I was barreling through Osborn's Corners, shifting gears on the twelve-minute drive home, in my mind I said, *I dare any cop to pull me over now because they're going to be delivering this baby*! I was in transition!

As I arrived home and roared up the driveway, I cranked on the emergency brake, and I made it to the house hunched over and holding my belly. I arrived at the door and said to Dean, "Just tell them to come!" I knew without a doubt that this was not false labour; the baby was coming.

Dean delivered our baby boy on our bed with Lyndsay and Kayla rubbing my back. My mom and the midwives looked on from the doorway. Derek was born at 4:28 pm.

It was truly a magical day, and the entire family gathered that evening at our home for a birthday dinner to celebrate the first grandson. Everyone was so happy, and Dad said, "Finally, one with a handle!" There were already four granddaughters on my side of the family, and my father-in-law was so thrilled to have a boy to carry on the Latimer name.

This day was the official start of my maternity leave. Just two weeks later, my dad was admitted to the hospital in Hamilton.

Tuesday, March 20th, 2001-Dad is Admitted to Hospital

Dad ended up with cellulitis and was admitted to the hospital forty minutes away. Those days were filled with many obstacles and challenges. My mom and I were at the hospital with him, to help when the nurses weren't available. It seemed like every single day there was more bad news. Dad was battling as hard as he could, but his body continued shutting down. It was heart-wrenching to see him bedridden when he had been such a strong, athletic, and active leader in our community. He was rapidly losing weight and having multiple adverse reactions to medications. It was gruelling for all of us. His body was always one step ahead of what the doctors were doing, and not in a good way. He couldn't eat because of the sores in his mouth, he couldn't drink, he would pull out his pic lines...it was just unbelievable what he went through, not to mention the hallucinations and the mental anguish for my mom and him. At one point he said to me, "Well this sure is terrible timing." I had a baby in tow. The truth of it was that Derek was a huge blessing and enabled me to be with my dad during that difficult time. Otherwise, I would have been in the office full-time and at home with my girls and Dean, and I just wouldn't have had the time to get to Hamilton.

Saturday, April 14th, 2001-My Birthday

I don't even recall my birthday.
Winter was ending in Ontario, and spring was dawning. My mom

was looking forward to the day my dad would be coming home, and she had everything ready for him.

Derek was just five weeks old, and I was still on my maternity leave. I was able to spend a little more time with Lyndsay, Kayla, and Dean. Our house was sold; we just had to finish packing up our home and taking care of all the details so that we could move. I continued to spend time with Dad, and of course, I was sleep deprived with having our new baby.

Monday, May 14th, 2001-Our Dream Home

What an exciting day! The keys for our new home were handed over to us. The house was empty for the week, and all the contractors were able to get their work done before we were to move in on the Friday. With everything going on, Dean and I were back and forth between the two houses all week, the girls were at the sitter's for part of each day, and I did not make it to Hamilton even once.

Friday, May 18th, 2001-Moving Day

The week certainly flew by. The movers delivered the girls' furniture, and all I had to do was make their beds. We decided to have their rooms painted identical to our previous home. It truly felt like home, and the transition was really easy for all of us. It was so nice to just get into bed that night and enjoy our new home in the country.

Saturday, May 19th, 2001-Dad was Stabilized

Dad called me from Hamilton at 6 am. Of course, if he was up, everybody should be up. He was so excited for us and the move that we'd made, and he wished that he could see our new home. We always valued the opinions of our parents, and included them when we were purchasing our homes. They all had viewed the property with us in January when we were considering buying it. I told him that it would not be long before he would be over to see it. He was stabilized now, and we were just waiting for him to build up his strength before he was able to come home. What a day that would be. He had called me because he wanted me to come down and give him an adjustment. I headed down as soon as I finished nursing Derek. We had a great visit, and I stayed most of the morning. We then spent the rest of the day trying to start the process of getting settled at home, unpacking, and catching up on a nap.

Sunday, May 20th, 2001-Laughter with Friends

Dad called Mom at 4:30 am to see if I could come back down again. He knew I was busy, but he had missed me over the last week (and I missed him too). All the time that he had spent in bed over the past nine weeks was hard on his body physically. I called him at 6 am and told him I would come down after lunch when the girls were napping. I had not seen the girls much that week either, and family time was important. Mom came to the hospital a little bit later, and some friends visited too. It was a great afternoon with lots of laughs and memories shared. When Derek and I left at 4:15 pm I gave Dad a kiss goodbye and said, "I'll see you tomorrow."

5:17 pm-Finally Free

Derek and I had barely stepped in the door at home when the phone rang. The nurse asked if I could immediately return to Hamilton as Dad was not doing well.

It turned out my dad was already gone. He was 57. His body had shut down completely with a massive heart attack, due to interactions with the medications. As I was racing back to Hamilton with Derek, I was always watching the highway to see if my mom was coming from the other direction so I could catch her on the way. When I arrived at the hospital and saw my dad all I could say was, "You are finally free." I was so happy that he was released from his suffering. I finally reached Mom at home, and all I could tell her was that she needed to come back to Hamilton. I could not tell her that Dad was already gone. She left immediately and refused to have someone drive her. I was able to have some close friends at the hospital for when she arrived, to help and support us. My younger brother was at work and was able to come right away, and our youngest brother was away for a long holiday weekend camping trip. Dean made the trip to bring our brother home.

One of the greatest difficulties was that my mom had never contemplated that Dad wasn't coming home. She had everything ready. The house, the yard, the pool; it was all ready for his return. She was completely and utterly devastated. It seemed like her world ended when her high school sweetheart left her.

While at the hospital I contacted a family friend who was a funeral director. I let him know that Dad had just passed, and I asked, "What is the next step?" I assumed that some arrangements had been made as Dad had been diagnosed four years prior, he had not practiced for six months, and had been hospitalized for nine weeks.

There were no arrangements made. We had to start at the beginning.

Every one of us has our own story, things left unsaid or undone. I cannot speak to the regrets that any of us may have had at the time of Dad's passing; all I know is that I felt like I had to support everyone during this time of huge loss because they were not just grieving, they were all suffering.

Next, we had to make the arrangements for my dad's funeral. Selecting a casket was quite the experience.

Thursday, May 24th, 2001-Dad's Funeral

The two days of visitation were a blur. I was still breastfeeding Derek while hundreds of people came to pay their respects. At Dad's funeral, I delivered his eulogy, with my voice wavering only once. I had not yet shed one tear for the loss of my dad. There was no time for that in my life. There was no time for me.

Monday, June 4th, 2001-Back to the Office

Life around me was carrying on as usual. I was now supporting all our grieving patients who were missing their friend, their doctor, and their mentor. I had not yet allowed myself to grieve. I had to hire an associate for the practice, as I could not do it all on my own. This added more stress and responsibility to my plate.

Saturday, August 25th, 2001, 7:30 pm-My Calgon Moment, NOT!

So here we are, the day of my health crisis when the events of the previous 302 days came crashing down on top of me.

I understand now that I was spared that day because my work here is not yet done, and I was to bring our son Jake into this world too. That event is when I realized to my very core that my husband and our three children are my 'why'. I was determined to not let my babies grow up without me as their mother, and I would not leave Dean on his own.

You may already know that any stressor in life, whether it be a happy or sad event, will take your body out of homeostasis, the balance that the body attempts to maintain 24/7.

It seemed that I had all major life stressors, good and bad, occur within the span of 302 days:

- An enormous shift in job responsibility, Dad was no longer able to practice
- Huge uncertainty surrounding Dad's health
- The increased physical workload while being four months pregnant
- Purchasing our new home and applying for a second mortgage
- Selling our home
- Packing
- Derek arriving three weeks early
- Dad being admitted to the hospital two weeks later
- Received possession of our new home, moved in, and lost my dad all in six days
- Back to work one week later

- Having to support my mom, my brothers, my children, my husband, my patients, my staff, and everyone else *except myself*

Do you think that I was working just a little too hard? That my life was a little out of balance? Do you feel this way some days too? I was Superwoman. I could handle it all, yeah right! My body started to shut down, and the time came when I had no choice but to listen. Sleeplessness, loss of appetite, dizziness, heart palpitations, missed beats, racing heart rate. This is what led to my health crisis. I was just thirty-three years old!

The big turning point was when my husband and our kids became my reason why, my reason to get balance back in our lives. It has taken some time, but we did it. We now have four beautiful children, I practice thirty hours per week, and I have incorporated me time (this is a hard entry in my calendar) into my life.

What I do know is that our bodies are amazing at adapting to our environment. They handle change without our even thinking about it, and inform us when things are out of balance. However, I have also learned firsthand that there is a finite limit to how much they can adapt. I had no choice but to listen to my body because, if I didn't, I wouldn't be here today. What I have learned is that self-love has everything to do with it.

When grief and feelings are buried, the body loses its balance. The funny part is that our body does give warning signs, and they do start early, but we often ignore them because we choose to not deal with them. We tell ourselves, "It'll go away on its own." If I had done just that when I was thirty-three, I would not have seen thirty-four, my husband would have been raising our three children on his own, and our youngest would never have been born.

It is much easier to correct a small problem than it is to turn around a major health issue, and for many, there is no second chance. As we know with heart attacks, they can come in an instant, and it can be over in seconds. I am one of the lucky ones.

Seventeen Years Later

Through these experiences, there are so many things that I have learned. It has taken years of study, trial and error, combining many techniques, protocols, and different teachings for me to be able to develop balance in my life, with self-love being the core concept of everything that I do.

I now begin every single day with me as the central focus because I have learned that if you don't take care of yourself, no one else is going to do it for you. Self-care is not selfish, it enables you to give more to all of those around you. Without your health and well-being, and when you don't take the time to nourish your mind, body and your spirit, you will suffer. You will live a life of exhaustion, you'll be overworked, overwhelmed, frustrated, and living a life that you don't love. When you take care of yourself first, you then will be able to recharge your batteries, calm your mind to a peaceful place, and enable your body to be strong physically. This allows you to give so much more to all those around you, those who you want to serve, and this then leads to you living a life that you love.

I have been blessed with being given a second chance, and I have dedicated my life to serving others. I love pouring my heart into my clients to support them, and I am here for you too. For a complimentary consultation please contact me at drstacey@drstaceycooper.com with the subject: LOVE.

Now that you know my story, you can see that it is quite evident that I did not have balance in my life. Can you relate to this too? How often do you feel like you can truly relax and be quite and still? Do you take time to be still? I didn't! There were many different kinds of stress and pressures that I allowed to be placed on me. And yes, it was I who did allow it. Now I know that I am in control of my experiences and I do get to choose. Join me in the next chapter, where I will share with you many ways to help quiet your mind, create space and time in your day, and reduce the stressors in your life.

When, If Not Now?

Record Your W.I.N.N.s Here

_____

_____

_____

_____

_____

_____

_____

_____

_____

_____

_____

_____

_____

_____

_____

_____

_____

_____

_____

_____

_____

_____

Chapter 10

Quieting Your Mind

No person, no place, and no thing has any power over us, for 'we' are the only thinkers in our mind. When we create peace and harmony and balance in our minds, we will find it in our lives.
—Louise L. Hay

1-Stress Reduction

Did you know that stress is a survival mechanism? Stress is your body's natural reaction to any kind of demand that disrupts life from the usual everyday stuff. When an event, either positive like a job promotion, or negative such as a job loss, occurs which takes you away from the balance point of homeostasis and your normal everyday living, your body responds with the stress response.

When you encounter a perceived threat, your body prepares to fight or to flee for your own safety. For example, when you encounter a scary dog, the physiology in your body changes in order to get ready to survive the encounter. Your heart beat will increase, along with your blood pressure, in order to feed your muscles oxygen so that you can be physically ready to meet the challenge. This is survival of the fittest. In small doses, stress is good — such as when it helps you conquer a fear or gives extra endurance and motivation to get something done. This scenario is usually short-lived, and then once the stressor is gone, your physiology returns to your resting normal, and homeostasis is once again achieved. This is what occurs when your stress response is working well. The issue arises when the stressor does not dissipate. When the stressor is present more often than not, and your body is in a near constant state of fight or flight, your stress response is out of control, and this is when your parts start to wear out. This is bad stress, which is often caused by worries which may include money issues, job performance, relationships or your health. Feeling stress for too long, whether for several hours, days or months, sets off your body's warning system. This includes not only physical symptoms but emotional symptoms too. Your body's stress warning signs tell you that something isn't right. This is just like the "check engine" light on your car's dashboard. If you let the signs and symptoms go unnoticed, you can run into a major engine malfunction. Stress that is left unchecked or poorly managed is known to contribute to many physiological degenerative conditions such as high blood pressure, heart disease, obesity, diabetes and suicide.

When you feel like things aren't going your way, and you are losing control and overwhelmed, pay attention to the warning signs, as they are just some of the ways that your body is telling you it needs to slow down, and would appreciate some extra care. Headaches, muscle tension, neck or back pain, upset stomach, dry mouth, chest pains, rapid heartbeat, difficulty falling or staying asleep, fatigue, loss of appetite or overeating "comfort foods," decreased immune function and increased frequency of colds, lack of concentration or focus, memory problems or forgetfulness, nervousness and jitters, irritability, short temper, and anxiety are all signs of your system working overtime and in a state of distress.

Do you notice that some of these symptoms may also be experienced when you consume too much caffeine? Caffeine is a stimulant, leads to increased cortisol levels in your body, and stresses your adrenal system. Cortisol is the stress hormone in your body, therefore consuming more caffeine either from coffee, tea or colas during times of increased stress is actually making the situation worse, and feeds into this negative cycle.

When you notice a stiffness in your back, or that you are snapping at your friends, pay attention to the signs and listen to what your body is telling you. While the adrenaline rush after acing that presentation to the board is something to enjoy, the warning signs of stress are not anything to take lightly or to ignore. By noticing how you respond to stress, you can manage it better and in healthy ways, which will help your body correct itself, thereby reducing the high cost and care of chronic, long-term health problems.

Mental attitude and general outlook play a role in how you perceive your life experiences, and also determines how you will react to that experience. This can be directly tied to your home life and upbringing, and will be influenced by your family and those who you model, but it does not stop there. The community you reside in, the culture of your upbringing, the people you meet, and the ideals that they expose you to also influence your behaviours and patterns. The music you listen to, the books you read, and the messages from the media that you are exposed to all affect your entire being. When you are bombarded by external influences it can become difficult to filter it all out. The best way that I know of is to first recognize an event as being stressful and to recognize when the early signs of your personal stress response begin to show up. Nipping it in the bud is the key to stress reduction.

One of the steps that you can take to help reduce the incidence of stress from occurring in the first place is to keep a positive attitude. If you perceive most situations from a negative perspective then the degree of severity of the situation will be dramatically increased from your point of view. However, when you perceive the same situation from a positive perspective, your stress levels will not be affected to the same degree. Remember that you are able to choose. Every single moment you have a choice as to how you will perceive, react and respond to every single situation and experience. If you want different outcomes, then begin to choose differently.

A key factor when you want to reduce stress levels is to realize and to accept that there are events in life that you cannot control. It is much less stressful if you can roll with it rather than get beat up by it. Being assertive instead of aggressive is another key concept. When you can assert your feelings, opinions, or beliefs instead of becoming angry, defensive, or passive, this puts you in the driver's seat, and you feel more in control rather than a victim of circumstance. Above all of these is the concept of relaxation techniques. These come in many forms, and it is important to try different ones and see which resonates with you most. You may find that particular ones work best for certain situations. Here are some things that you can try. Meditation, yoga, or tai-chi are great for stress management. Exercising regularly is of great importance, as I will share with you in Chapter 11, and your body can fight stress better when it is fit. Eating healthy, well-balanced meals is important for decreasing nutritional stress and for fuelling your body better. Learning to manage time more effectively will reduce stress levels dramatically. Setting limits appropriately and learning to say 'no' to requests that would create excessive stress in your life is a very powerful self-love tool that I shared with you in Chapter 2. Making time for hobbies, interests, and relaxation is vital for balanced living. Getting enough rest and sleep will ensure that your body gets the time it needs to recover, repair and restore from stressful events. Spend enough time with those whose company you enjoy, as there is nothing better than a good laugh to lift spirits and reduce stress levels. Laughter truly is the best medicine.

2-Meditation

The physical, emotional, and spiritual benefits of meditation have been well documented for thousands of years. Meditation is disconnecting from an activity and letting yourself drift into the space between your thoughts. Did you know that there is space between your thoughts? I know there was a time that my life was moving so fast that it did not seem like there was any space between any of my thoughts, and there probably wasn't because I certainly know that there was no space for me in that part of my life. Practicing meditation has changed this for me, and it can for you too.

Just like any other skill, meditation is a practice, and it does take practice in order to develop this skill. Read on in Chapter 11, where I share my story of how I got started with yoga and meditation. Let me just say that I did not take to it like a fish to water, and it was some time before I truly appreciated it.

In the Yoga Sutras, written sometime between 200 b.c. and 200 a.d., meditation is defined as "One-ness is the progressive quieting of the fluctuations of the mind."

As you begin a meditation practice, over the first few days, weeks, and months of daily meditation, you will notice the quieting impact which this simple practice has on your bodymind. (Yes, bodymind is not two separate entities, as the body and the mind are interdependent and do function as one and do influence each other so I will be referring to the bodymind here.) Your bodymind begins to express itself in each choice you make. Over time this makes a huge impact on your overall stress levels and therefore the function of your body. Your shift may be so subtle that even you don't see these meditation benefits at first. But your thoughts, decisions, choices and daily actions become more conscious, leading to more intuitively conscious behaviours, then one day you realize you have a broader perspective, a deeper sense of calm and heightened clarity, expanded grace, and greater ease. You realize you are making more spontaneous right choices. You realize you are being more authentic. There is greater alignment between what you think, what you say, and what you do. These are the myriad effects and benefits of meditation. The world is still turning—and sometimes faster than ever—but to you, that swirl is in slower motion, like texts coming into your cell phone with a really faint hum rather than a blasting ringtone.

Over time, moving from activity to stillness during meditation translates into more conscious behaviours during non-meditation (the other 23 or so hours of your day). Your interactions with the world shift more effortlessly from reactivity to responding, from reflexiveness to reflectiveness, from defensiveness to openness, and from drama to calm. This is a true reduction in your stress levels as your mind quiets.

There is a big bonus regarding the effects of meditation, on top of all these other nourishing aspects. Over time, meditation benefits you by quieting you to a state where you experience life with a deeper understanding of your true self, which can open the door to spiritual exploration, connection, discovery, and fulfillment. This is one of the many spiritual benefits of meditation. It is along the so-called "spiritual path" that you truly can experience your unbounded and unconditioned Self. This is the infinite you that rests at the core of who you are underneath your body, and is your true inner being.

Regardless of the depth of your spiritual nature, simply by spending time in stillness and silence, you will experience the benefits of meditation and become more imbued with the ability to open to greater possibilities in each moment instead of the ones you were fixed on.

This creates a more universal trajectory for the rest of your life, with an expanded point of view. By seeing yourself as more universal and less personal, you'll realize more options in each moment, instead of seeing only the limited ones you thought you had before. Everything in your life becomes richer when you see that there are lots of different ways things can play out, and your previously constricted viewpoint only made you feel more helpless as life unfolded. But this tool called meditation and its benefits can give you the edge you need to feel strong each day, to gain clarity, and to finally regain your peace of mind. A few minutes of practice per day can help ease anxiety. "Research suggests that daily meditation may alter the brain's neural pathways, making you more resilient to stress," says psychologist Robbie Maller Hartman, PhD.

As you begin your journey into mediation, you do not need anything special. Simply find a quiet place and you can sit in a chair or on the floor. Sit up straight and if on a chair sit with both feet on the floor. If on the floor, sit with legs crossed. Close your eyes and focus your attention.

When I first started meditating, I used a guided meditation. There are many resources for this, including one that I recorded for you, which you can find on my website under the 'podcasts/interviews' tab at DrStaceyCooper.com . Using a guided meditation is a helpful tool to keep yourself on task as you are starting out. Following the 'story' that is created in the guided meditation is great for relaxing your brain and reducing stress. When meditating on your own, reciting a positive mantra either out loud or silently is helpful to keep your mind from wandering and being 'busy.' Examples of a positive mantra are "I feel at peace" or "I love myself." Use whatever resonates with you at that moment in time. Place one hand on your belly to synchronize the mantra with your breath. Let any distracting thoughts float by like clouds.

If you are just beginning, my suggestion is to start with 5 minutes. Set a gentle timer so that you can truly sink into the moment and forget about watching the clock. Then get into a comfortable, quiet space and begin to relax. Now focus on the guided meditation and follow every word that is spoken, or recite your mantra. Stay focused on the meditation, and when the thoughts of the day float into your mind, acknowledge them and then release them so that they may be on their way out of your mind. Enjoy the meditation and remember that with practice it will become effortless. In the beginning it may be easier said than done, but with practice you will see amazing changes.

3-Relaxation And Creativity

Quieting the mind is a critical component in order to enjoy total relaxation of your being, and taking time to slow down in this crazy, fast-paced world is vital.

How often do you actually think about how you breathe? I know that your body is so incredible that you do not have to think about breathing, but do you know that there may be many times throughout the day when you are barely breathing and certainly not nourishing your body with oxygen effectively? Your lungs have a huge capacity for transporting incredible amounts of oxygen to your body, but with a sedentary lifestyle, as well as chronically increased stress levels, you may find that you are not breathing well at all. As you are breathing right now notice if your chest is moving very much. Does your abdomen move in and out with each breath? Or perhaps you do not notice much movement of your body at all as you breathe. I dare say that this is more typical than not.

I have touched on the importance of breathing in regards to the delivery of oxygen to the cells throughout your body in order for energy to be produced and utilized, and now I will share the importance of using your breath to actually slow down all of the other systems in your body.

I invite you to try out this exercise with me. When it is convenient, I ask that you take a 5-minute break with me and focus on your breathing. In order to do this, just sit up straight and then gently close your eyes and place your hand on your belly. Now slowly inhale through your nose. I would like you to become aware of the sensation of breathing. Feel the breath come in through your nose and travel downwards. As the air comes into your lungs they will expand, and this will then force your abdominal organs downwards and your belly will move outwards. This is belly breathing. Reverse this process as you exhale through your nose. Use your abdominal muscles to gently push the air out of your abdomen, up through your body and out through your nose. Repeat this belly breathing, allowing the air to pass only in and out of your nose. Deep breathing counters the effects of stress by slowing your heart rate and lowering blood pressure.

Another form of relaxation is by allowing your 'thinking' brain to take a break while engaging your 'creative' brain. Just like physical exercise, creative stimulation engages and focuses your mind on the task at hand, and it distracts you from feelings of stress and anxiety.

When you create, you invoke your imagination, which is a productive and constructive use of your mind. By focusing intensely on a creative task, you can achieve the state of "flow," the term coined by psychologist Mihaly Csikszentmihalyi, and which is typically defined as the "optimal state of consciousness where you can feel your best and perform your best."

In other words, when you "lose yourself" in the composition of a song or the creation of an artistic piece, or in drafting a poem or story, you are essentially entering a healthy flow state. You do not notice time or events happening around you. According to acclaimed author Steven Kotler, during periods of flow, your brain secretes a healthy dose of pleasure-feeling chemicals such as dopamine, serotonin and norepinephrine. By creating, you may enter flow, which can give you a rush of good feelings. You may experience positive feelings because creation is ultimately an act of freedom where you manifest the world you want to see, one music note, one paint stroke, or one rhyme at a time.

It has been discovered that individuals who are more creative tend to live longer, presumably because creativity stimulates many brain regions which in turn keeps it healthier.

"Individuals high in creativity maintain the integrity of their neural networks even into old age. Keeping the brain healthy may be one of the most important aspects of aging successfully," said Nicolas Turiano, a psychologist who was one of the researchers. He also noted how creative people tend to handle stress better, because they tend to reframe potential obstacles as opportunities instead. "Creative people may see stressors more as challenges that they can work to overcome rather than as stressful obstacles they can't overcome."

When you are feeling down and out, get busy and creative. By putting yourself into a creative state, you will be swapping negative feelings out for positive ones, and perhaps crafting a masterpiece in the process.

Many other ways to incorporate relaxation into your day can include taking even just 10 minutes to decompress, perhaps with a Progressive Neuromuscular Relaxation Session (available for free from my website under the podcasts/interviews tab) or with a warm cup of tea, or even just closing your eyes. A massage is another way to remove physical muscle tension from your body.

4-The Space Between Stimulus And Response

Physiologically, it is important to allow all of your systems to come to a resting idle and to be quiet in order for them to be able to replenish, regenerate, and repair. This does not just hold true for your mind, which may spend a lot of the time racing, but it is important for your entire body as well.

To explain how this works, I would like to share a quote from psychiatrist and Holocaust survivor, Viktor Frankl: "Between stimulus and response there is a space, in that space lies our power to choose our response, in our response lies our growth and our freedom."

In other words, there is a moment of choice before you react to the stressors in your life. However, you may be unaware of this space "between stimulus and response" because of your habitual patterns of reacting to life.

Let's walk through an example in order to illustrate this concept. Imagine that you are driving along a busy highway. As you are cruising along minding your own business, a car cuts you off on the highway and you have a thought, "What is wrong with that guy?" Your heart has already begun to beat faster due to the perceived stressful situation of a car accident. Your hands also begin white knuckling the steering wheel. Anger boils within you and feeds your thoughts about how the other driver needs to be taught a lesson. Perhaps you speed up next to him to stare him down, letting him know that you know what he has done.

This is stressful and a highly unpleasant situation fuelled by the ongoing, and unconscious, interaction between your thoughts, feelings, emotions and your behaviour. I would argue that there was no choice in this situation because the driver was unaware of the stress reaction that you had; however, there was a space or maybe even spaces in between the moment he cut you off and your reaction.

Becoming more aware of your habitual reactions will help you to interrupt this cycle and create more choices in life. Maybe upon reflection you will realize that reacting to the driver who cut you off that way only increased your stress and did not make a difference to the other driver. So in the future you may become more aware of your reaction by noticing your hands white knuckling on the steering wheel or your heart racing, alerting you to the stress reaction occurring. In that moment you are present and are sitting in that space between stimulus and response. You then get to take a few deep breaths, let your shoulders relax a bit, and even consider the unpleasant state the other driver must be in to be driving that way. Perhaps you may even wish him well, because if he was, he wouldn't be driving that way. As you begin to become aware of this and begin to practice pausing between receiving a stimulus and providing a response, you can begin to realize that you can break through long-held fears that have held you back from living the life you want to live. Also, when you take these few very precious moments to pause between stimulus and response, your stress levels will decrease dramatically, and as you continue to implement this practice in your day to day events, your entire outlook on life will shift to a much more positive perspective.

As you have learned, everything in the body is connected, and as you start to shift towards a more positive perspective, your entire being will become healthier because your physiology will be changing as well. With a more positive attitude, your daily stresses will seem less stressful, and with deceased stress levels your heart rate and blood pressure will decrease too. Many other systems within your body will also be positively affected, and this will contribute to the reversal of degenerative diseases.

I encourage you to accept that there are events throughout your day that you cannot control. The key is to not let them get the best of you, but for you to be the best you through those negative events by being assertive instead of aggressive. Assert your feelings, opinions, or beliefs instead of becoming angry, defensive, or passive.

Now that I have shared with you in this chapter easy tips for helping to quiet your mind during a hectic day, check out the next chapter where I show you how to do the same for your physical body so that all of your systems can come to a resting idle in order to replenish, regenerate and repair for optimal health.

When, If Not Now?

Record Your W.I.N.N.s Here

_____

_____

_____

_____

_____

_____

_____

_____

_____

_____

_____

_____

_____

_____

_____

_____

_____

_____

_____

_____

_____

_____

Chapter 11

Quieting Your Body

It takes courage to say yes to rest and play in a culture where exhaustion is seen as a status symbol.
—Brené Brown

1-Rest

Restoration of your body is a crucial component to healing and health. Every waking moment of every day results in millions of cells in the body being utilized, metabolized, destroyed and discarded. If this were to continue indefinitely, it would not be long before there were no more cells left in your body. This is why cellular restoration and repair must occur daily, to enable your body to continue to function the next day. There are cells in your body that do have a finite life span. Did you know that your red blood cells die after 120 days? Your body will regenerate a new skeleton every seven years. You actually have cells in your body to do all of these functions, to build up tissue, to break down tissue, to remodel tissue, and to discard old tissue. The whole system works in harmony, but harmony can be lost when time for restoration is not present. Your body can only go through its housekeeping and cleanup phase when it is not occupied doing all of the other activities of daily living. This means that it can only do it during rest. When your body does not receive adequate rest, this repair phase cannot take place.

Now you may think that, when I am talking about rest, I mean sleep. Sleep is a very important factor in the health of your body, and many people struggle with good sleep. Some of the things that you can do to improve your sleep patterns can be very simple, while others require a little more preparation. I will tell you that the old wives tale of drinking a cup of warm milk before bed will not help you to sleep. The fact is that when you eat too close to bedtime, your body gets confused. When you eat, your body will send the majority of your blood flow to your abdomen in order to be able to process the food that you ate, and distribute it throughout the rest of your body for energy production. When you are sleeping, your body is concentrating on repairing tissues and systems throughout your entire body. When you eat right before bed, your body doesn't know what it is supposed to be doing. So one of the first things you can do to help your sleep is to stop eating at least a few hours before bedtime.

Another useful tip is to tire out your body. A weary body will crave rest, and this is why exercise is a great component to aiding in a healthy sleep pattern. Exercise creates energy in your body so I do not recommend that you exercise right before bedtime as you may actually then find yourself staring at the ceiling with lots of energy running through your body.

Having a regular bedtime is helpful because your body can get into a routine. If you find that you are waking up before your alarm goes off each day, this is your body clock at work. The same holds true for going to sleep. When you maintain a consistent time for sleep, than it will be easier for your body to fall asleep at this time of day.

There have been many times when new moms have come into my office seeking advice about how to help their young child go to bed easier. I always suggest a night-time routine. Now this does not just hold true for infants, as everyone's sleep mechanism is similar. It works for adults too.

Things that you can incorporate at bedtime include ceasing the use of any electronic device at least two hours prior to sleep time, and never taking your phone to bed with you. With your phone at your bedside, you are never truly asleep as your subconscious is always on alert just in case that important call comes through. All phones are equipped with call answer, so shut the thing off and get some much needed rest. The other factor is the light emitted from the screens, which actually changes the sleep-wake cycle in your body because the pineal gland in your brain is stimulated by the light. Because your body naturally works on the circadian rhythm and the light-dark cycles, when you are exposed to intense light prior to sleep time, your body believes that it is daytime and that you should be awake. This is of great hindrance to a restful sleep.

Taking time to be quiet for an hour or 2 before sleep time is also helpful. This may include such things as going for a walk in the evening. The fresh air and connecting with nature can have a very calming effect. It is also useful for bringing muscle relaxation to the body, as blood is flowing throughout your tissues while you walk. Another thing you can incorporate is reading a novel for entertainment, not studying for a test. Studying before bed will actually get your mind racing, and may stress it as you are thinking of the test the next day. Reading a novel will help to shift your thoughts away from the stresses of your day, and will leave your mind thinking about the storyline. This is a great way to quiet the mind, give yourself a break from stress, and aid in a more restful sleep. You may find that taking a soothing hot bath may be helpful for relaxing your body as well.

A restorative yoga session is also a wonderful way to bring relaxation to your body, and therefore will aid in a more restful sleep. You may find that by doing Child's pose (as explained in Chapter 12) has many benefits and is great to do before bedtime. While in the pose you are concentrating on the pose instead of the grocery list or other thoughts that may be racing around in your head, and you are also in a naturally relaxed position as your head is down in a dark space and you are not as stimulated by the lights and noises around you. This helps to relax you, and brings a calming to your system which will then aid in sleeping.

2-Yoga

Yoga is not to be feared, even though I admit that I did not like it the first time I tried it. Do not be scared and do not think that you have to be a young girl who can contort her body like a pretzel in order to be able to do yoga. This could not be further from the truth.

When it comes to quieting the body, yoga is one of the best practices that I have found. I did not always feel this way. I have always been an active person, and when I first tried yoga I was impatient and did not know how to quite my mind. I was used to doing aerobic classes and step classes and I was very much on the go always. I did not stop for anything. I first tried yoga about 18 years ago, when I was expecting Derek (our third born). When we were to lie down at the beginning for the meditation, I was thinking about the grocery list, who was to go where next, what I needed to do for tomorrow, and on and on. That is the headspace I was in. When we started the poses, I followed the directions of the instructor and got into the pose, then I could hear myself say; "Ok, I'm done that one, now come on! What's next? Hurry up! I'm ready here!"

Yoga is not about what others are doing. It is about you and only you. You do not need to be able to turn yourself into a pretzel. You do not have to be able to touch your toes. Yoga is all about you, listening to your body and working within your limits. An excellent yoga instructor will always guide you into a pose and will also provide alternate poses if needed. I have been practicing yoga for the past 10 years, and have come a long way from that first yoga class where I was so impatient. Now I look forward to the quieting of my mind, and the meditation sessions which are part of yoga practice. It has also enabled me to gain flexibility, strength, balance, and greater mental clarity.

The act of practicing yoga is over 5,000 years old. Monks used the postures to stretch out their bodies because they would spend hours and hours sitting in meditation. (Read on in Chapter 12 where I share with you the importance of stretching.) Just think, if you were to spend 1/2 an hour sitting cross-legged on the floor, your legs would get tired, your muscles would cramp, and you would get spasms. So the monks devised the postures which are called Asanas so that they could stretch their bodies and make themselves more comfortable so that they could sit for longer periods of time.

Yoga is actually a sanscript word that means to "yoke" your body, your mind, and your breath. Yoga looks at your whole body and your whole lifestyle.

You may be asking, "So why should I try yoga?" I will share with you some of the incredible benefits that I have received since practicing Yoga. Yoga helps to increase your breath. Increasing the prana in your body helps to enhance your vitality. You will feel better, and you will process things better in your body when you increase your breath. When you put your hands over your mouth, and you are trying to breathe in and are not getting a full breath, your body is not circulating properly, and it is causing you decreased energy levels. When you take a deeper and fuller breath you feel better, and your body will function better as energy production is dependent on delivery of oxygen to your cells.

Yoga also helps to improve your balance, your flexibility, your posture and your health. Working with the balance poses becomes a way of life. When you are standing at home, for instance, and working in the kitchen, you can raise a foot up and balance from side to side. Or if you are waiting in line at the bank or grocery store, you can lift one foot and then the other. Here you are incorporating poses and practicing your yoga throughout the day, not just on the yoga mat. This will help to improve your balance. The more you utilize the neurological pathways within your body, the more ingrained they become and the stronger your reflexes become. This is incredible training for your system. As you age, pathways become used less as a more sedentary lifestyle is experienced, and this is how balance deteriorates as you age. If you continue to utilize these pathways and keep them strong, you will maintain your skills and your balance will be improved.

When practicing yoga your flexibility will increase. You will find that you can pick up that piece of paper off the floor more easily. Practicing yoga will also help to improve your concentration. Focusing on quieting your mind and bringing it to stillness helps to improve your concentration.

Yoga also helps to improve your circulation, your digestion, and your mood. Sometimes when you are in a sad mood, if you do a yoga practice for 10 or 15 minutes, you will feel that shift in mood, and you will feel lighter afterwards. Yoga has also been used to reduce anxiety and aid in depression.

There are a number of yoga styles and practices that you can find on the market right now. One you may not be familiar with is Chair Yoga. I invite you to join us for a chair yoga session. Just go to https://youtu.be/6s-u714u32w as my dear friend and my personal yoga instructor Rosemary Lee has provided a short introduction to chair yoga. This is a short session designed for all ability levels, and one of the best things about this session is that you can take it with you anywhere. You can do it at your desk at work, or wherever else you might be. In this session you will use a chair for support, and the yoga postures are modified so that you can participate easily with a chair. Chair yoga is actually harder than you think, because you are using different muscles to perform the different postures. When you are at your computer, you can take a 5 minute break and do some of the chair yoga practice rather than pulling out a mat and getting on the floor. Now you can actually get some movement into your body during the day by doing the postures in a chair.

When you begin to participate in yoga I do recommend that you begin with an open mind. As with anything, you can jade your experience of something new by allowing your past experiences and preconceived notions to taint what is new and un-experienced. Please check your "educated" mind at the door, come in with an open mind, and allow yourself to enjoy the experience. Be willing to try something new. Yoga is about being in the now! It is not about the grocery list, obligations, or the stressor of your day. It is not about worries or concerns. It truly is a quiet break for your body and your mind.

3-Exercise

It is a common fact that exercise is important for many aspects of healthy living. Some of these factors include the health and tone of all of the muscles of your body, not just those of your skeleton. Did you know that your entire digestive system is made up entirely of muscles? When your activity level is decreased, your digestive system function can become slow and sluggish. If you spend the majority of your day sitting, your blood flow will be decreased, and your muscles will be weak. This includes the muscles of your digestive system too. All of the muscles of the body would benefit from a workout throughout the entire day, and this leads to enhanced physical body function.

When considering why exercise is important for your body, I would like you to think of some reasons why you think exercise is important for you. I know that as I begin to move my body during exercise, I experience increased blood flow throughout my body, and it makes me feel better because I am utilizing energy and this gets the engine running. During exercise your body will also release hormones called endorphins which are a natural painkiller. Exercise not only stimulates muscle function and joint mobility, but it also aids in clearing the mind, and is therefore a great stress reducer which absolutely helps in quieting the body.

There are many healing benefits of exercise. Your body adapts to the environment that you provide, whether that be positive or negative. When you are sitting at home, achy and stiff, and feeling that there isn't any possible way that you could exercise, you will continue to feel achy and stiff. If all you do is sit in a chair, it will not take long before that is all that your body will be able to do. Now do not get discouraged. Just as your body adapts to this inactivity, it will also adapt to new activities. All you have to do is start! Just start by taking a few steps. Start by walking for only 5 or 10 minutes if you are not used to walking for extended periods. Whatever it is, just start!

Listen to your body and progress at your own rate. With every single day it will get easier, and you will start to feel the benefits of your workouts.

Your heart rate, lung function, blood flow, and cardiovascular system all benefit from exercise. Strengthening of muscles and also strengthening of bone occurs through exercise, and this reduces the incidence of osteoporosis too.

Now let's see where you are starting from. This is for your own personal grounding. When setting goals for your health it is important to know where you are starting from in order to know where you want to go. I ask you to take some time now to answer these questions for yourself.

• I think that exercise is important because...
• Some exercises that I ENJOY and would like to include in my routine are...
• The best part of the day for me to exercise would be...

You will be able to begin to implement your responses into 'The Plan,' which I will discuss in Chapter 14.

It is really important that, when you begin an exercise program, you make sure that you are doing something that you enjoy! If you hate jogging, do not decide to jog, because you have already set up your first roadblock to being successful. Pick what you like. That way you will enjoy it, look forward to doing it, and you will then actually want to exercise.

I asked you to think about the best part of your day to exercise. For me it is morning. If I do not get it done then, it doesn't get done. The day can get away on you, and before you know it, it is time for bed and you did not exercise. I find that if I do exercise at the end of the day, right before bedtime, I am charged up and will not sleep as well. I will also switch it up. Sometimes I will do a yoga session, then an aerobic workout the next day, then cycling, then weights, then cardiovascular. Doing this will keep your body from getting into a training rut, and will keep your mind active too. When you have a number of different things that you enjoy doing, you will not get bored. You can just choose to do what you feel like doing that day, as long as you get active and move your body. Typically the length of my workouts will vary as well, depending on the intensity of the workout and how much time I have that day. On Wednesdays and Fridays I am not tied to a schedule; they are 'My Days' and I can work out longer. Exercise is what I call a "hard" entry on my calendar. We are going to be talking about that later in Chapter 14, when we cover the CLEAN™ Living Formula. Exercise is a hard entry on my calendar, but the length of time will fluctuate, depending on the day and what exercise I am doing. My exercise does get scheduled because if it is not on the calendar then it doesn't happen. Just like a dentist appointment, chiropractic appointment, work schedule, or anything else, it s important to schedule exercise. You can develop an active and healthy lifestyle by including a few simple things into your daily routine. Be sure to get adequate rest so that your body can repair and restore. A balanced diet will give your body the fuel it needs to be re-energized. A little bit of exercise will go a long way. Start off from where you are, even if it is by walking down the block. It is important to slowly build up your endurance over time, and not overdo it as this will result in you being discouraged and will hinder your progress.

Going for a walk will get you off the couch and out of the house. You will enjoy some fresh air and sunshine, and will begin to burn some calories, which will give you more energy. It will give you time to clear your mind, get your heart pumping and your lungs working, decrease your blood pressure and cholesterol levels, increase your endurance, and improve your quality of life.

As you can see, quieting the body does not just entail chilling out and watching television on the couch. In fact, if you do that too much, your body will actually become more tense instead of less tense, and this defeats the purpose of what you are trying to accomplish with relaxation. Check out the next chapter, where I share with you some incredible facts about your body and what just 'sitting around' does to it.

When, If Not Now?

Record Your W.I.N.N.s Here

Chapter 12

Stretching

Whatever kind of workout you settle on, it should include the Big Three of exercise for health and fitness - aerobics, resistance exercises, and stretching.
—Jane Fonda

1-The Detrimental Effects Of Sitting

It is a common belief that exercise is important, but some may think that it has to be going out for a jog, working out at the gym, or lifting weights. These activities do provide many benefits to your body, but all of these activities also lead to increased muscle contraction. In regards to improved function of your body, it is actually more important to stretch your body, in order to experience enhanced joint mobility and muscular relaxation, than it is to strengthen your body. This is because through stretching, and activities like yoga, you are using your body weight to perform the stretches, and you are actually strengthening your muscles and your skeleton at the same time.

This fact may surprise you, but yoga and calisthenics are almost on the same playing field. The only thing missing from yoga is pull-ups, in regard to a workout routine. Other than that, every other muscle group gets a full workout through yoga poses, because you are working against the resistance of your own body weight. I have patients who have increased their skeletal bone density, as determined on a bone scan, by eliminating all dairy products from their diet and by incorporating yoga into their daily routine.

In a previous chapter when I asked you about how much time you spend sitting in a day, were you surprised at how much time you actually spend sitting in your day? Had you ever stopped to think about that before?

Staying in one position over an extended period of time leads to degeneration of your physical structure. Sitting at a desk all day can cause great fatigue, even though you felt like you did not do anything physical. The reason for this is that your small postural muscles have spent the entire day holding you up. Just think if I were to ask you to hold up a 10 pound weight in a bicep curl for 1 hour. Would your body succeed at that? No I expect not, unless you had trained to do this. Your body would give out as your muscles would fatigue, and you would then drop the weight. That is exactly what you have demanded of the little postural muscles of your neck. They have been contracting all day long to hold up your 10 pound head! This has required great energy from your body, and has placed the postural muscles in a contracted state for extended periods of time. The result is a feeling of fatigue, with no desire to engage in exercise, and this leads to tightening and compression of the joints. Generally when you are standing, the muscles are in a lengthened position, but when you are sitting they are in a shortened, contracted position. In a sitting position the hip flexors, the calf muscles and the hamstrings are all in a shortened position, in order to allow the knee to bend. As you sit, you tend to hunch forward and your shoulders round. This leads to contracture of the pectoral muscles in your chest. If you are working at the keyboard your fingers are also flexed, contracted, and tight. This leads to tightening of the joints, decreased range of motion, loss of function and mobility, and degeneration of the joints.

Muscle contraction, even when sitting, requires energy. And of course, exercise requires energy too. This energy expenditure in either situation leads to fatigue. This is why in the evenings when you think that you should go to the gym for a workout, you feel like you have zero energy in order to do so, even though you did nothing strenuous all day. Perhaps all you did was sit at your desk all day. Just by sitting, you have become fatigued. Now you have an even lower desire to exercise. You are so exhausted, how could you even go out and do anything?

If you are not stretching, your muscles stay in the shortened position, and they just get tighter because they never get stretched out. This leads to tightening of the joints because now you are muscle bound. This results in decreased range of motion. When you are experiencing decreased joint function, you will have a loss of function of the body which leads to degeneration. You do not have free movement, you do not have normal blood flow to the area, the muscles are not stimulating the joint, and it starts to deteriorate and get compressed. This is when you start to seize up like the Tin Man in the Wizard Of Oz, and you are in need of an oil can. Please see the Diagram of How Sitting Leads To Joint Degeneration on the next page.

Now let's get back to the question of how much time you spend sitting during the course of a typical day. When you wake up do you sit down to eat breakfast? Or perhaps you eat breakfast while sitting during your commute to work. How much time do you spend sitting while on your commute to and from work? Do you sit at work all day long? Or perhaps you perform repetitive tasks and make the same motions with the same muscles over and over, until it is time to sit for the commute home.

The point is that in your daily life there are many parts of the day when you are sedentary. Another factor to consider is that, due to the energy saving mechanisms in your body, you will also be dominant on one side of your body, either right-handed or left, but generally not both. Generally you will pick up the heavy grocery bag with your dominant hand. You will also tend to lead with the same dominant leg every time you go to walk up a flight of stairs. All of this leads to increased muscle development on one side of the body, and weakening on the other side, and this leads to imbalances in the body. The result is overuse syndromes where there is excessive contracture in one muscle group over another, and this leads to joint dysfunction. I will discuss this principle later in this chapter.

Sitting = Joint Degeneration

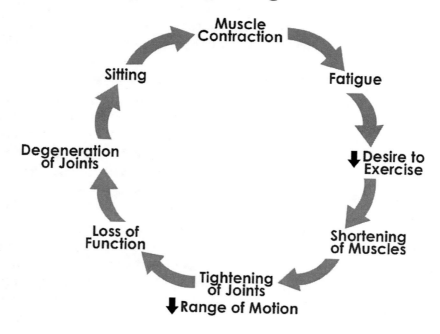

2-The Benefits Of Stretching

Stretching offers many benefits throughout your entire body, not just for your muscles and joints. The ideal scenario would be for you to spend equal amounts of time stretching in the opposite direction to the position you are in all day long. What I mean by that is that if you find yourself sitting in a chair all day long, then you should be stretching your body in the opposite direction to open up the chest and the lungs, and to straighten your legs and reduce the strain on your spine. This would then provide balance to the muscle structure of your spine and your entire body. This is not practical as there are not enough hours in the day to sit for 8 hours and then to stretch for 8 hours. That is why it is important to incorporate stretching throughout your day. This will help to stave off the tension and tightness, because you can stretch the muscles before the severe tension sets in.

Stretching will not only improve mobility and decrease fidgeting, but will also improve blood flow to the starving muscles, decrease tension, improve function and help to balance your spine and body.

With the amount of time that is spent sitting, the hamstrings gradually get stronger and tighter until they start to pull the pelvis down with them. This is called a posterior pelvic tilt, and it changes the curvature of the spine.

There are 3 curves to the spine: the cervical lordosis, thoracic kyphosis, and lumbar lordosis. When the hamstrings are tight and they start to pull the pelvis down with them, this results in the lumbar lordosis flattening and creates weakness and dysfunction of your spine, because these joints are now working in a fashion that they are not designed to. They are supposed to function along a gentle curve; that is how they were designed. When you increase a curve in your spine, the muscles then become shortened in the area; they are contracted, and this leads to more joint compression which equals joint degeneration.

Another example is when wearing shoes with an elevated heel. When your foot is placed in such a shoe, all of your weight is shifted forward from your heel onto the ball of your foot. It is not the high-heeled shoe that is supporting you, but rather the shortening of your calf muscles in your lower leg. In this situation the calf muscles are constantly in a state of nearly full contraction as the toes are essentially pointing downwards, depending on the height of the heel.

Static stretching is a technique where the muscle is slowly stretched and then held in the stretched position for several seconds, so that a greater length of the muscle can be achieved. This is the most frequently used and most recommended type of stretching. There is a low risk of injury with this technique.

I recommend that you start off with 3 sets of each stretch, and increase as your ability increases. Whenever you are starting something new, start slow. Do a few and see how you feel the next day. How many times have you gone out into the garden for 3 hours and thought, 'This is great! I feel fantastic!' and 'I could do this every day', only to wake up the next day feeling like you will not be able to move for 3 days? The best test is to see how you feel the next day. If your body responds well, you can gradually increase the number of sets. If you can "feel it" the next day, then continue at this level for a period of time (a few days, or a week) to allow your body to build its strength, ability, endurance and flexibility. Slow and steady will win the race, and will also prevent injury. You do not go out and run a marathon without training. If this is a new activity for you, be kind to yourself and start slow. This will also help to ensure your success because if you work within your body's tolerance you will be able to continue with the program. When you overdo it, it will take a few recovery days before you will want to resume your program, and at that point you may lose your motivation to do it at all.

Stretching your muscles and reducing tension throughout your body will result in an improvement of your body function, which will then help to restore normal spinal curvatures as well as improved function of the joints, and will reduce degeneration.

The bottom line is, if you want to stay pain- and injury-free, having a strong body is only part of that battle. Having a mobile body is essential.

3-The Effects Of Strengthening

Every skeletal muscle in your body crosses a joint. Muscle contraction is what causes joints to move and enables you to have motion. Muscle strengthening is important to maintain proper function of the body; however, if the body is not strengthened equally for all of the major muscle groups, imbalances occur which can lead to abnormal wear patterns of joints, and joint degeneration. How Muscle Tension Leads to Joint Degeneration is illustrated in the diagram on the next page.

When you have balanced muscle tension on all sides of a joint, your function is normal across the joint surface and you will experience normal joint motion. When the muscles on both sides of a joint are not strengthened to the same degree, there is dysfunction of the joint motion. This leads to compression on one side of the joint compared to the other, which with the passage of time leads to abnormal wear on the joint surface and creates degeneration within the joint space. Just think of when your car needs an alignment and the wear on the tires is uneven. Strengthening just the weak group of muscles leads to more muscle contracture (or shortening of the muscle) and more joint compression.

Unbalanced Muscle Tension Leads to Joint Degeneration

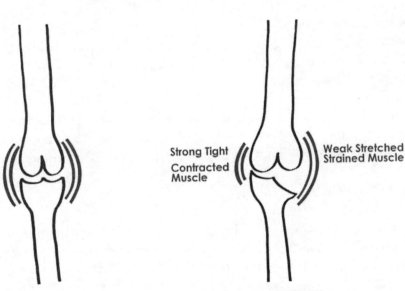

Strong Tight Contracted Muscle

Weak Stretched Strained Muscle

Balanced Muscle Function = Normal Joint Motion

Stretching Muscles = Improved Joint Function

Unbalanced Muscle Tension = Joint Dysfunction and Leads to Joint Degeneration

Strengthening the weak Muscle = More Joint Compression

As you can see in the diagram, a normal joint has equal space from side to side along the joint line, whereas the other joint shows joint narrowing on one side, and joint gapping on the other side because of the muscle imbalance. Think of the muscle like an elastic band. When it is tight on one side, this brings the 2 bones closer together. The other side then has to give a little as it stretches, and this causes this side to have a gap.

When you drive your car and the tires are not aligned, how is the wear pattern? It will be uneven. The same thing happens here. When you are putting more pressure on one side of the joint, the cartilage that is in between the bone, the nice little padded cushion, will begin to wear out as it is being squished and stressed. It will degenerate and dry out, and the result will be a very painful joint with bone rubbing on bone. What is the end result? A new knee, perhaps, through knee replacement surgery. However, this surgery cannot be performed at too young of an age because the new knee will only last so long. A different approach is to take measures to ensure that the joints last longer in the first place. Prevention is the key. Is it not better to have and maintain better body function and not to have to replace the knee in the first place?

When you focus on fixing the muscle imbalance, or if you do not let the muscle imbalance happen in the first place, you will not end up in this situation. You will have a balanced, normally functioning joint.

4-The Importance Of Mobility

The hip flexors in the front of your pelvis and upper leg are considered the tightest muscle in the human body, due to the fact that the average person spends up to 40 percent of their life in a seated position. If the time spent sleeping is 1/3 of your life, and another 40% is spent sitting, then no wonder the body gets stiff and tight.

Something else you may not have considered is your fingers. You may not spend much time thinking about your hands but they do spend a lot of time in flexion from typing, writing, eating, driving, etc., and this tends to cause them to curl.

Stretching for every region of your body is important, and to increase your range of motion is simple in theory, but it is not easy in practice. It requires concentration and patience. Additionally, not every stretch is appropriate for every individual. Some people will naturally be tighter in some places of their body, while others will achieve a full range of motion with little effort. If you are not tight in a given area, you may not feel any need to stretch there at all. I have seen a handful of adults who can comfortably get into a full butterfly stretch or lotus pose without really working at it, even though these same folks are sometimes tight in their upper back or hamstrings. Every person is different as we all use our bodies differently depending on our jobs, our activities, and our history of trauma and injury. There are certain circumstances where specific stretches may actually be contraindicated or harmful for certain individuals. For example, a person with a lower-back injury may exacerbate that situation if they engage in excessive hamstring stretching because generally it will be the tight hamstrings that are causing the low back issue. When they start to stretch the hamstrings, and if they do so too strenuously, this can actually have the opposite effect to that which was desired. Another person with a frozen shoulder may have trouble with moves which require placing the arms overhead. This is why it is always important to listen to your body, work within your tolerance, and do not cause any pain. Stretching is meant to be comfortable and relaxing, not painful or creating injury.

You can generally work up to improving function in any joint of the body no matter where you are starting from, as long as you listen to your body and work within your abilities. In these situations always progress slowly, or modify some of the poses to better suit your individual needs. As I often remind my clients and my patients, you have to listen to your body and work within its limits. While the spectrum of mobility of the body amongst individuals is quite diverse, we all have the potential to achieve a full, healthy range of motion in all of our joints. Certainly there are some folks who may naturally be tight, but generally the cause of most people's stiffness is years of neglect in a sedentary lifestyle. Your body adapts to your actions (or inactions). If you move often, you will get good at moving, but if you spent most of your life sitting in a chair, chances are your hips, hamstrings, shoulders, and upper back have tightened up as a result. It takes a long time for this to happen, and it can take just as long to undo. If you have been working for 10 years at a desk and then you think that 2 weeks of stretching at 5 minutes a day is going to change things dramatically then you are mistaken.

In Chapter 15 I share with you a story of how joints that have been immobilized for as little as 4 weeks can take up to 3 months to become mobile again. I encourage you not to have unrealistic expectations. It will take time, and it will be worth the effort; just don't expect to magically improve your range of motion without any effort.

You will gain some immediate benefits by implementing stretches into your day, and you may need to give extra time and attention to certain areas of your body. I also recommend that you try to avoid activities which negatively affect your particular situation.

5-The Benefits Of Improved Flexibility

The practice of stretching should be the most valuable part of your physical training, but I do recommend that you not get too attached to the idea of achieving any specific goal. What I mean by this is if you are just beginning a stretching routine and you have not participated in one for a long time, I do not recommend that you hold the expectation that you will be able to touch your toes in two weeks time if at present you can only reach down as far as your knees. Progress is fun and encouraging, but those feelings of excitement can be fleeting. No matter how far you come in your training, there are always new skills and poses to work toward or refine. Keeping a humble, joyous attitude about your training is the healthiest way to achieve long-term growth.

Static stretching can be an effective means toward improved flexibility and enhanced mobility, which can then be a means toward improved functional strength.

Many people neglect working on their flexibility. This does not only decrease their quality of life, but it can also cause injuries due to lack of range of motion. For example, those who have problems putting on their shoes and tying them will benefit from increased flexibility. People who play sports or work out will find that they have improved athletic performance and fewer injuries when they work on improving their flexibility. Those who do have good flexibility will also have much better posture. Posture is extremely important for body function. If your posture is poor, and because we generally function in an upright position all day long, the result will be increased tension in the neck which can contribute to headaches, as well as decreased lung function and decreased cardiovascular function. This is because with a slouched posture your ribs are compressing your lungs, preventing them from expanding fully. You may also experience abdominal upset because now there is decreased motility of your intestinal tract. Poor posture has far-reaching effects on many systems within your body.

Your body becomes accustomed to whatever stimuli it is repeatedly exposed to, so the more regularly you stretch, the more mobile you will become.

Did you know that by improving your flexibility you will also help repair minor muscle tears by stimulating increased blood flow to the tissue? The blood delivers oxygen and nutrients to the tissues, and it also stimulates muscle growth.

It is quite possible that you will discover a lot about your body when you begin stretching. If you have injuries or structural impediments (such as artificial parts in your body from joint replacement surgery) then be sure to contact your health care provider and only exercise within the range of motion that your body can tolerate.

To improve your mobility it is also important to train your core. It may sound funny, but a strong core allows you to be more mobile. When the spine is stable, the hips and shoulders do not need to hold stabilizing tension, and this allows them to move more freely. You will have greater mobility of your hips and shoulders if your core is strong.

Flexibility is also joint specific. For instance, the shoulder is the most moveable joint in the body. It is a ball and socket joint. You can move your shoulder in more directions and it has more range of motion than any other joint in the body. Try to move your toe in the same fashion that you can move your arm for an arm circle. Your toe does not move that way. In contrast the knee joint can only move in 2 directions, flexion and extension. If it goes in other directions, this is a bad thing. Extension of the knee is limited physiologically through its particular joint mechanics, so be sure to work within the physiological tolerances of your body.

When working on restoring function to an injured area, be sure to contact your primary health care provider for specific guidance. In general, be sure to use gentle motion for rehabilitation, and do not push the end range. The goal is to enhance function, not create more damage, so be sure to work within the limits of your body, and very gently challenge it as you go.

6-Full Body Stretching Routine With Youtube Link

When stretching, it is very important to breathe. Holding your breath during a stretch will tense your muscles, and this defeats the purpose of what you are trying to accomplish in the first place. Instead, you can encourage relaxation by exhaling longer than inhaling while you stretch. This enables you to breathe into and relax into the stretch. You will find that you will then be able to stretch just a little further. You want to slowly get to a position where you feel slight tension, take a deep breath in and then let the breath out as you position into the stretch and then be sure to relax. It is important to not 'tighten' into the stretch but to actually 'let go' as you move into the stretch. Hold the position and continue to breathe. Before you finish the stretch, try going just a little deeper into the stretch. You never want to go to the point where you feel pain, as you never want to rip or tear your tissue. Be sure not to "bounce" during the stretch. Stretching should be a slow and gentle activity with the simple intention of loosening your muscles and improving your flexibility.

It is recommended that you stretch at least three times a week. You want to stretch 10% beyond normal length only if your body is capable of that, or to the point of tension. You can hold the stretch anywhere from 10-30 seconds. You should ideally try to achieve between 3-5 repetitions.

Now is the time to put words into action. I am providing you with a full head to toe stretching routine that you can begin to implement right now. As an added bonus you can view my full video demonstration at the link: https://youtu.be/6xZ-qjK8AKo.

Remember that slow and steady will win the race, and will also help to prevent injury from occurring. You would not go out and run a marathon on day 1 without any training, would you? Well, as for any new activity, you need to begin where your body is capable.

It is my recommendation that you start off with 3 sets of each stretch, and be sure to do the stretches in both directions in order to balance your body.

Begin by standing with your feet hip-width apart. Have a slight bend to your knees in order to tuck your pelvis under and protect your back. It is important to contract your abdominals in order to keep your core strong, and be sure to continue to breathe.

If you are sitting, both feet should be flat on the floor, not cross-legged. Work within your abilities, listen to your body, do not cause pain, and just go to the point of tension and hold it in order to allow the stretch. If it hurts or causes pain then back off a little bit or eliminate that exercise until your body is functioning better.

All of the stretches are written here with a complete description as a reminder of how to do them. For my complete video demonstration just go to https://youtu.be/6xZ-qjK8AKo and follow along with me.

- **Neck Rolls**- Chin to chest, ear to right shoulder, chin to chest, ear to left shoulder. Never go backwards.
- **Neck Range of Motion**- Look left and hold. Look right and hold.
- **Shoulder Rolls**- Bring shoulders up to ears, backwards, and then press them down. This is one cycle.
- **Forward Shoulder Rolls**- Bring shoulders up to ears, forwards and then press them down. This is one cycle.
- **Arm Circles**- Slowly and gently make big circles backwards with your arms.
- **Forward Arm Circles**- Slowly and gently make big circles forwards with your arms.

- **Touch fingertips together behind your head/back**- Reach the right arm straight up beside your ear. Drop the right hand down behind your head with right elbow bent. With the left arm, place it behind your back and attempt to touch the fingertips of your right hand. Use a hand towel if you are not yet able to reach your fingers.
- **Finger Press**- Place hands in front of you in prayer position. Try to have heel of palms touching each other, fingers straight and elbows parallel to floor.
- **Wrist stretch**- Outstretch right arm and let wrist drop. With left hand encourage more stretch of the right wrist. Repeat with left wrist.
- **Side Bending**- Slide right hand down the right leg towards right knee and hold. Feel the stretch through the left side of body. Hold for 5 - 10 seconds. Breathe. Repeat on opposite side and then repeat the set 3 times. For an advanced stretch draw the top arm over the head in line with your ear.
- **Waist stretching**- Place hands on hips and swing the hips slowly in a circle while pushing the boundaries. Repeat in the opposite direction.
- **Quadriceps stretch**- Hold on to a chair for stability if necessary. Grasp right ankle with right hand and draw heel towards buttock. Hold. Repeat on the other side.
- **Lunges**- Place hands on hips or hold on to a chair for stability. Place right foot forward and be sure to always be able to see your right toes. Work towards keeping left heel on the floor and feel the stretch in the front of the left hip. Repeat on other side.
- **Side lunges**- Use a chair for stability if you need to. Place feet in a wide stance and shift over to the right side and feel the stretch in the left inner thigh. Repeat on other side.
- **Calf stretch**- Stand facing the wall and with outstretched arms place hands at shoulder height on the wall. Keep heels flat on the floor. Lean in towards the wall to feel the stretch in the calves (Imagine a standing push-up position). Variation: In Lunge position, keep heel on floor and open stance until you feel stretch in the calf. Or yoga pose of "Down Dog" or "Dancing Dog."

- **Ankle circles**- Point the toe and write the alphabet in the air. Repeat with other foot.
- **Squat**- With feet hip width apart, try to keep your heels flat on the floor and squat. Try to have the hamstring muscles rest on the calf muscles. This will stretch calves, hamstrings, gluteals and lower lumbar spine.
- **Lumbar Stretch/ Knee to Chest**- Laying flat on your back with legs flat on floor. (Lay with knees bent and feet flat on the floor if necessary.) Bring one knee to the chest and hold for a count of 10. Breathe and relax. Let that leg down and bring the other knee to the chest and hold. Then bring both knees to the chest and hold. Repeat.
- **Knee stir**- Laying on your back bend right hip and knee to 90°. Grasp right knee with both hands. Imagine using your knee to stir a pot clockwise. Repeat in the other direction. Repeat with other knee. Great stretch for low back and the sacroiliac joints.
- **Mid thoracic stretch**- Laying flat on the floor, pretend you are on the rack. Point your toes, place your arms beside your ears and let the backs of your hands rest on the floor. Stretch through the entire length of your body and hold for 10.
- **Child's pose**- Get on your hands and knees on the floor (Table pose). Keep your hands stationary and push yourself backwards to sit on your heels. Reach your hands forward on the floor ahead of you and attempt to place the forehead on the floor. This will stretch and open the lumbar spine and stretch through the shoulders, arms and chest.

Child's pose has many benefits and is great to do before bedtime as you would then be concentrating on the pose instead of the grocery list or other things racing through your head. You are also relaxing as your head is down in a dark hole so you are not as stimulated by lights and noises around you. This helps to relax you, and brings a calming to your system which will then aid in sleeping.

Calisthenics and yoga are closely related. There is a lot more overlap between basic bodyweight exercises and fundamental yoga poses than most people realize. Yoga is just another form of bodyweight training.

Though yoga places more emphasis on flexibility than the modern calisthenics tend to, you can certainly build strength through yoga practice. Just think of the body builders who are muscle bound and have limited range of motion.

Muscle contracture = joint dysfunction & decreased range of motion.
Yoga = improved flexibility and better body function.

Balance is very important for better body function, and it is dependant on the functioning of a complex neurological pathway. As they say, "If you don't use it you lose it!" The same holds true for your neurological system. If you do not continue to stimulate the pathways, they will not function as efficiently. Think back to when you were a young child. Perhaps you liked doing somersaults under water, spinning on the ice in your figure skates, or spinning round and round on the playground. Your body, over time, would accommodate to those spinning patterns, and then you would be able to do them with ease and not get dizzy. If you have not done that particular activity for a long time, years even, and you tried to do it again today, I dare say you would get quite dizzy and probably even fall down. In order to keep the system functioning well, you need to continue to repeatedly run that 'neurological highway' and keep the road clear. When you stop performing a task, that pathway is no longer a well-worn highway, but becomes an overgrown trail with roadblocks, and then the information will not get to where it needs to go and you will lose your balance.

You can practice your balance even while you are standing at the sink. Be sure to have something to hold on to, and be conscious of what you are doing. When you are standing on one foot, your body is making thousands of minute corrections in order to keep you upright. Alterations are being made every single microsecond. Muscles are contracting on one side and relaxing on the other in order to keep you from falling over. All of this information goes from your ankle to your brain and back again to make the corrections. That is how the body works.

As you implement this stretching routine and include balance exercises into your daily activities, it will not be long at all before you begin to see changes in how your body functions. As your flexibility increases, you will have a greater ease of movement. As your balance begins to improve, you will have less susceptibility to injury.

As I discussed in Chapter 3, your brain is the computer of your body and tells everything what to do and how to do it. Therefore communication from your brain through your nervous system to every single cell, organ and system is vital in order for your body to function optimally. Read on to learn more about how you can enhance the function of your computer.

When, If Not Now?

Record Your W.I.N.N.s Here

_____

_____

_____

_____

_____

_____

_____

_____

_____

_____

_____

_____

_____

_____

_____

_____

_____

_____

_____

_____

_____

_____

_____

_____

Chapter 13

Chiropractic Wellness Care

I appreciate health care that gets to the root cause of our symptoms and promotes wellness, rather than the one-size-fits-all drug-based approach to treating disease. I love maintaining an optimal quality of life naturally with Chiropractic.
—Suzanne Somers

1-What Is Chiropractic?

I had realized at a very young age that chiropractic was not only part of my family history since 1912, but it was also my personal calling. At the age of 12 I was spending Saturday mornings in the office with my dad helping out at the front desk. It truly was remarkable to me to be able to see the healing ability of the body happen right before my eyes. Some patients would come into the office not even able to walk under their own power, and after their chiropractic adjustment with my dad they would be able to walk out of the adjusting room without help from others. To this day I am still in complete awe of the innate healing ability of the body, and of how my ability through my chiropractic training and using my two hands, along with the incredible chiropractic adjustment, I am able to remove interference from the nervous system in order for the computer of the body to be able to communicate with every single cell, organ and system to unleash the innate healing potential within the body.

Chiropractic is a natural, non-invasive form of health care without the use of drugs or surgery. Chiropractic care deals with the cause of the problem, not just the symptoms.

My purpose as a Doctor of Chiropractic is to empower you with knowledge as to how your body functions, and to educate you as to why you may feel the way you do. I help you to learn why your body is doing what it is doing, so that we can get to the cause of the problem and resolve it in order to allow you to experience better body function, not just pain relief. I also do not only consider the area of where pain may be experienced, because that is often not the cause of the problem, but rather is often just the symptom. I practice wholistically because nothing happens in isolation within the body. Many of my patients have commented that I need to hang another shingle on the door because healing is not segmental, it is not regional, and it is not isolated. If you have other stressors going on in your life that are not being dealt with, they will express themselves physically. Chiropractors can adjust you physically, but if the stressor that is causing your situation is emotional, the problem will persist. Often it is when patients are face down on the adjusting table, and they don't have to look at anybody, they are able to open up, and a lot of emotional healing occurs.

Everything within the body is connected to and communicates with everything else via the nervous system. Your nervous system is the computer of the body, and regulates every single cell, tissue, organ and system. Because of this remarkable setup the body is a miraculous adaptive mechanism. Your body is able to adapt to whatever situation or environment you provide for it. This is survival of the fittest. Did you know that during reproduction, after the egg and sperm unite and the initial cellular multiplication and division occurs, the very first system of the body to form during embryonic development is the nervous system? It is the most vital of all of the systems of the body, as it is the master controller. Without it there is zero function. Without function there is death. The nervous system monitors your internal and external environments and makes fine tuning adjustments to all of the systems of your body, to adapt to the existing environment. This occurs 24/7/365. The nervous system is responsible for you being able to breathe and for your heart to beat without you giving it a thought at all. Without breath and a heartbeat there is no life. Therefore the nervous system is the controller of life.

Because the nervous system is so vital to living, it is completely encased in bone for its protection. Your skull and vertebral column are the armour of the nervous system; however, there are times when the bones can hinder its function.

This situation is called a vertebral subluxation and is corrected by a chiropractic adjustment.

When any of the 24 vertebrae of the spine become misaligned, the delicate nerve roots that exit the spinal column between every single vertebrae can become impinged upon. This leads to decreased function of the nerve, and the information which travels along the pathway of the nerve is interrupted. The result is that whatever is at the end of the nerve (a system, an organ, or a cell) does not receive the proper information, and dysfunction is the result. This leads to the expression of symptoms.

There are limits to the adaptation process of the body, and when those limits are reached, this is the point at which signs and symptoms begin to appear. By the time the symptoms begin to appear, the cause of the problem has been present for quite a long time. The reason why you did not know the problem was present was because your body had been trying to cope with the problem on its own, and now the body cannot tolerate the problem any longer and the symptoms are telling you this. In order to avoid symptoms from developing, the cause of the problem must be corrected. A Doctor of Chiropractic is specifically trained and educated to locate and correct the spinal subluxation which is causing the nerve interference. Chiropractic care plays a very important role in helping the body to function optimally and to be symptom free. You do not need to live in pain. Pain is only a symptom which lets you know that the body is not functioning properly, and that the cause of the problem needs to be corrected.

You also do not need to have symptoms present before you consult with a Doctor of Chiropractic. The reason for this is that your body has a remarkable ability to adapt to many different situations, and it can adapt a lot before symptoms and pain become evident. Symptoms and pain are the body's way of communicating to you that something has gone wrong, and that you need to get it looked after. For the most part there is always a reason for something happening in the body. It did not just get there all by itself, so it cannot just go away all by itself.

2- The Chiropractic Adjustment

Doctors of Chiropractic are primary health care practitioners. Our extensive training in diagnosis and symptomatology equips us to be able to diagnose everything and anything that walks in our door. As such you do not need a referral to attend a Chiropractor.

After a chiropractic consultation and examination, when it is determined that a patient would benefit from chiropractic care, they would receive a chiropractic adjustment.

An adjustment is a skilled, gentle, specific maneuver which is performed only by a Doctor of Chiropractic to re-align the position of the vertebra in order to remove the interference to the nervous system and to restore joint function and normal nerve communication throughout the body. The result is not only the relief of symptoms, but correction of the cause of the problem.

The purpose of an adjustment is to restore the normal alignment and motion of the joints of the spine. All joints are designed to move, and it is when they stop moving that problems arise. When the bones of the spine are misaligned or have lost their normal range of motion, this is called a subluxation. In order to experience better body function the subluxation of the spine is corrected by the chiropractic adjustment.

For those who "adjust themselves" if that worked there would be no need for Chiropractors. This difference is that Doctors of Chiropractic with extensive training are able to detect which joints are not functioning well and address the issue specifically. Therefore the affected joint is corrected. Those who "adjust themselves" are not able to correct the affected joint specifically, and therefore they seem to have to "adjust" themselves continuously because they are not correcting the specific joint that is causing the issue.

You may have wondered about the sound that is created during an adjustment. Rest assured that it is not joints cracking or bones breaking. It is actually the result of fluid attraction. Every joint consists of two bony surfaces which are bathed in fluid. Just think of an engine in a car and how it needs to be lubricated in order for the parts to work smoothly. Now imagine a glass sitting on a wet glass table. This resembles two hard surfaces which are bathed in fluid—like a spinal joint. When you pick up the glass you will probably hear a sound which is caused by fluid attraction. This same principle holds true when a joint is adjusted. The chiropractic adjustment helps return your spine to optimum health by restoring and maintaining nerve and joint function.

When an adjustment is given, it introduces a change into the body. After the adjustment, your body will slowly return to its original abnormal position because it is used to being there. The adjustment is required on a regular basis until your body learns to accept the new normal position. As your body begins to hold the adjustment longer, this is when function will improve and when healing can begin.

Once you experience how much better your entire body functions while under chiropractic care, you will want to maintain your good health. Regular spinal check-ups with your Doctor of Chiropractic will help to prevent the original complaint from flaring up, and aid in maintaining your improved body function.

3-The Benefits Of Chiropractic Care

When the nervous system – the computer of the body — becomes irritated, pain is not the only symptom. If your computer is not operating properly, everything along that nerve pathway can be affected. This includes symptoms like nerve pain, muscle spasm, joint irritation, as well as organ dysfunction and dysfunction of systems. In order to restore proper function, adjustment of the joints of the spine helps to restore their proper motion and removes the interference to the nervous system. If the nervous system is working the way it should be, the proper information can reach every single cell of the body, body function will improve, and symptoms will be relieved.

If the nervous system becomes aggravated often enough that you are experiencing symptoms on a regular basis, this can become a chronic situation. As the saying goes, "The squeaky wheel gets the grease," so listen to your body and get things looked after quickly so that it does not become a chronic problem.

The best suggestion is to be able to prevent symptoms from occurring in the first place. The body was not designed to live with pain on a regular basis. It is important to have your nervous system tuned up on a regular basis, just like going for wellness checkups with your other health care practitioners like the dentist, and the optometrist. By maintaining the health of your spine you will experience improved health and be on your way to becoming symptom free.

A question that I am asked frequently is "When should chiropractic care begin?" My answer is "Well before the symptoms turn into a chronic problem." Remember that pain is one of the last symptoms to develop, and that the problem has been present long before the pain began. Did you know that regular spinal check-ups can also help to prevent the problem from recurring, enabling you to maintain a healthy, active lifestyle?

The chiropractic adjustment helps return your spine to optimum health by restoring and maintaining nerve and joint function. Through the aid of the adjustment there is first a calming of the entire system, and many first-time patients report that after their first adjustment they had the best sleep they have had in years. Another comment as all of the joints begin to move more freely is that immediately after an adjustment the range of motion improves. Most notable is the fact that driving is much easier because shoulder checks are improved.

Every bump, fall and slip on the ice, every rollercoaster ride, bouncing on a trampoline, talking on the phone, spending time at a computer, driving in a car, everyday stressors, all of which many look like they would not cause any physical damage to your body, are truly detrimental to the optimal function of your system.

I do not know of anyone who would not benefit from chiropractic care, simply due to the fact that we live on earth with the force of gravity pulling down on us every second of our life. This alone causes stress to the spine and nervous system. Also, every single stage of life challenges your body and can have ill effects on your spine and nervous system. This is what I will cover in the next section.

4-The Benefits Of Chiropractic Care During Pregnancy

Pregnancy is the beginning of a whole new life, and is supposed to be a joyous, wonderful experience. Chiropractic care can help ease the discomforts of pregnancy, labour, and delivery, in a gentle effective manner.

During pregnancy a women's body goes through many changes in order to provide a safe and healthy environment for the baby to grow. With the changes in hormone levels, nutritional requirements, and body weight distribution, a woman can become uncomfortable or feel not at all like herself. As a pregnancy progresses and the baby grows, the physical shape of the mother's body changes dramatically. Her centre of gravity actually extends to a point in front of her physical body, and this places added stress on all areas of her spine, including the joints and the muscles. There is a shift in the curve of the lumbar spine, and the joints have to work differently than how they were designed. This will affect function. Chiropractic care can help to ease many of the discomforts of pregnancy. Safe and gentle chiropractic adjustments to the spine and pelvis allow the nervous system to function normally, and restore optimum joint mechanics, thus improving body function. When the body is working properly, it is much easier for a woman to provide a healthy environment for her growing child. A well adjusted spine and pelvis also set the stage for a much shorter labour and easier delivery of the baby, as the muscles and joints will be working more efficiently.

Also with my fellowship and training with the International Chiropractic Paediatric Association, I am also schooled in the Webster Technique, enabling babies to shift from a breech presentation. Generally babies present in a breech position because of intra-utero constraints. With this technique the pelvis becomes balanced, and this enables the baby to turn on its own. That is why this method is far more successful.

Chiropractic care is safe throughout pregnancy, during labour, and after delivery. Doctors of Chiropractic have special techniques that help a woman feel comfortable during every stage of pregnancy. I was adjusted throughout my four labours as well. When the pelvis is well aligned, this allows for the largest opening for the baby to pass through without any compromise. This produces a much more effective labour, with less resistance as well as an easier delivery. I do not know of any expectant mother who would not love to have a shorter labour and easier delivery.

5-The Benefits Of Chiropractic Care For Infants And Children

The birth process can be the most traumatic event in a person's life, depending on the interventions utilized. Traction on the head during birth may at times be necessary, but it can also cause tremendous strain to the spine and nervous system. A gentle chiropractic adjustment can correct the function of the spine, reducing nervous system irritation, and prevent chronic problems from developing. The best time to begin chiropractic care is in the very beginning of life, in order to ensure that the baby has a healthy, happy start.

Babies go through many physical challenges, even within their first few days of living on the outside of their mother. Even on the inside there are physical challenges. During the last three months of the pregnancy the area that the baby is growing into is getting smaller and smaller, and the baby has less room to move and stretch. This generally leads to the baby being in an awkward position for an extended period of time. You may notice that newborns often sleep with their head resting in an unusual position or turned to one side. This is probably the position that the baby was in during the last stages of pregnancy. This is not a normal position. The muscles of the neck and spine will be stretched a little more on one side compared to the other, and will be a little tighter on the other side, causing an imbalance in the spine. The neck of an infant can also be injured during the delivery process, especially if traction, forceps, vacuum extraction or a cesarean section delivery were utilized.

Common ill-health conditions of infants which may respond to chiropractic care include: irritability, colic, constipation, recurring ear infections and some respiratory conditions.

The spinal column goes through many changes throughout the course of development. At birth there is only one curve present in the spine. Once the infant begins to gain control of the postural muscles of the neck, and is able to hold the heavy head up, the second curve of the spine develops. It is not until the toddler begins to stand that the third curve of the spine forms. Now enters more trauma to the spinal column. Every tumble that a toddler takes results in compression of the spinal column on a very regular basis. Not to mention all of the other traumas that a spinal column will endure as a child grows (falling, bike riding, rough-housing, ice skating, etc.). If the impact and stress that the spine has suffered is not corrected by a chiropractic adjustment, the body has no choice but to grow in this abnormal position. "As the twig is bent so grows the tree." The result is decreased function of the body, and there is then the expression of symptoms at an early age.

The growth of the skeleton and spinal column is complete by 16-18 years of age. After this there is no further growth, so this system must then sustain the body for the rest of its existence, which can amount to 82-84 years if we are expecting a 100 year life span.

Common ill-health conditions of children which may respond to chiropractic care include: bed wetting, clumsiness, recurring ear infections, frequent colds, growing pains, headaches, painful joints, poor concentration, postural problems, and stomach aches. As we have determined, it is much easier, cheaper and more enjoyable to stay healthy than it is to go through crisis care. If prevention is the key, then chiropractic care from birth is the answer in order to maintain better body function.

6-The Benefits Of Chiropractic Care For Seniors

The majority of the population believes that with aging comes the suffering of aches and pains. This does not have to be the case. As you age, your body does slow down in metabolism and in the restoration process, but if you maintain an active, healthy lifestyle, your body will serve you well in the years to come.

Your body was designed to move, and if you keep moving your body will keep moving for you. The phrase "If you don't use it, you lose it" certainly applies to the body. If you just sit like a couch potato, it will not be long before that is all that your body will be able to do. Recall your body's miraculous ability to adapt to the environment that you provide. This is a prime example. I found this out first-hand when I injured my hand. With it only being casted for 4 weeks, I had lost complete and total function of my hand, and it took more that 3 months to restore the mobility.

If you have a car, you will know that taking it to the mechanic for regular maintenance, oil changes, and wheel alignments will help to keep it running longer for you. Maintenance is the key when you want your investment to run well for you. The thing is, you can always replace a car but you only get one body. When you place the same demands on your body physically day in and day out, this puts imbalance in your body. Visiting your Doctor of Chiropractic is just like taking your car to the auto mechanic. By getting a chiropractic adjustment you are realigning the joints of your body, restoring normal motion, reducing physical tension, and improving body function. It is not as easy to replace your body as it is to replace your car, and maintenance is the key.

Adjustments for seniors are of great benefit because the musculoskeletal system plays an important role in maintaining health and independence as we age. As you age, pathways become used less as a more sedentary lifestyle is experienced, and this is how balance deteriorates as you age. Proper function of your musculoskeletal system is important for also managing chronic conditions like diabetes and heart disease, because staying active and mobile is important for reducing the incidence of these degenerative diseases. Yet, we know that the prevalence of musculoskeletal conditions tend to increase with age and can seriously affect your health, quality of life and independence. A poor functioning musculoskeletal system typically leads to increased injuries due to falls. Bad falls can often lead to hip fractures and surgery, and this significantly impacts quality of life and can often lead to death. Therefore preventing falls is critical. Chiropractors, as part of your healthcare team, can help address musculoskeletal injuries early to help maintain mobility and function. Healthy aging relies on your ability to keep moving, and enjoying activities of daily living with little pain or limitations. Chiropractic adjustments may help to reduce pain, increase range of motion, and improve function. Did you know that the adjustment may also help to decrease progression of joint degeneration? Just like keeping mechanical parts such as a ball joint well greased, it is important to keep your joints healthy and functioning well with the adjustment.

As the body ages and postural muscles tend to tighten, you may notice a change in your posture. With being adjusted, you will find that your posture improves. When your spine is straighter you will feel better. This will enable your whole body to function better because when you stand up straight, your ribs are better aligned and now your lungs can actually function better. As your lung function improves, the delivery of oxygen to your bloodstream is more efficient, energy production at the cellular level will occur more effectively, and you will experience enhanced vitality. The adjustment has far-reaching effects on the function of your body. It also reduces physical stress and tension in the body, and may help to restore postural imbalances, thereby enhancing your balance. Maintaining physical balance and steadiness is a key component to reducing the risk of falling. As you can see, chiropractic care has many more benefits than just reducing back pain and relieving headaches.

7-Why Prevention Is Important

As you get comfortable in your daily routines, this places repeated stresses on your body that you may not even realize, and it leads to imbalances in the spine and nervous system. We are creatures of habit, and tend to use our bodies in the same way every single day. Once you become conscious of these actions you will notice things like: always putting your pants on the same way, always putting your shoes on in the same order, always leading with the same foot when going up steps, always carrying a bag on one side of the body. These are just a few examples. Most of us are also dominant on one side of the body. I am predominantly right-handed, you may be left-handed, but relatively few people are equally dominant on both sides. This one-sided dominance leads to imbalances in muscle development and strength from one side of the body to the other, and this adds stress to the spine. From different traumas and injuries the body will tend to age, and as a result of decreased function you may tend to become more sedentary and experience aches and pains. There are many different types of stressors which affect the body. Physical stress such as everyday housework, desk work, lifting, gardening or even sleeping on the couch can result in a strain to the spine and nervous system.

Other stressors include falls, accidents, whiplash, and sports injuries. These stressors can result in strains to the muscular system and result in pressure to the nervous system. When the nervous system is irritated, symptoms begin to appear.

Symptoms are the body's way of letting you know something is wrong. Symptoms such as headaches, back pain, neck stiffness, pain in your shoulders, arms or legs, numbness in your hands or feet, or nervousness are the most common signs of stress and dysfunction of the nervous system.

The reason that your body ages is not just due to the passing of time. What actually happens is that every trauma to the body causes aging. Every time there is an injury, repair has to occur. Whenever there is a symptom, that means that inflammation was present and repair has to occur. Any time cells and tissues have been damaged, repair has to occur. The original organized and strong tissue has been damaged, and repair occurs through the creation of a scar. Scar tissue is disorganized and weak. This sets the stage for more injury and degeneration.

After an injury, it is repaired with scar tissue. Because this 'new' tissue is weak, it is more susceptible to re-injury. When the next injury occurs it will be to a greater degree, the symptoms will be worse, it will take longer to heal, and it will be even more susceptible to re-injury. This is how the body ages. This is preventable!

If you keep your body moving and have your spine checked regularly by a Doctor of Chiropractic, this will not only help to alleviate aches and pains but will also ensure greater mobility and result in improved quality of life, as there will be less injury and therefore reduced degeneration and aging of your body. This will result in better body function.

When an adjustment is given, it introduces a change into the body. After the adjustment, your body will slowly return to its original abnormal position because it is used to being there. The adjustment is required on a regular basis until your body learns to accept the new normal position and begins to hold the adjustment longer, so that the healing can begin.

Once you experience how much better your entire body functions while under chiropractic care, you will want to maintain your good health. Regular spinal check-ups with your Doctor of Chiropractic will help to prevent the original complaint from flaring up, and aid in maintaining your improved body function.

Having your spine adjusted regularly will remove any interference that your nervous system is experiencing, and will allow your body to utilize its energy in the most efficient manner. The adjustment helps return your spine to optimum health by restoring and maintaining nerve and joint function. This helps to alleviate pain and tension, making you feel more relaxed and productive, and may enable you to sleep better at night. All of these benefits allow you to live a happier and healthier life, and enable you to live life to the fullest. For more information about chiropractic please visit my site at http://CooperChiropracticCentre.com

Now that I have shared with you the foundation as to how to support your body nutritionally, mechanically, and physically, and how to support your mind through relaxation, meditation and stress reduction, the time has come to share with you in the next chapter how I nourish all aspects of my life through balanced living.

When, If Not Now?

Record Your W.I.N.N.s Here

_____

_____

_____

_____

_____

_____

_____

_____

_____

_____

_____

_____

_____

_____

_____

_____

_____

_____

_____

_____

_____

_____

Chapter 14

Balanced Living

The balance you seek is not just between work and home or family, but also between work and home or family and you.
— Jack Canfield

1-What Is Balanced Living?

Balance as defined by the Oxford dictionary is an even distribution of weight, enabling someone or something to remain upright and steady.

I would like you to reflect for a moment and consider how often you feel steady and upright. Is this how you feel the majority of the time? Or do you rarely feel this way? Is your life travelling at such a speed that you feel like you can never catch up, that you are just holding on tight and wishing for the ride to slow down? Do you feel as if you are being constantly pulled in multiple directions and wish there were more of you to go around?

Balance is also defined as the stability of one's mind or feelings: the way to some kind of peace and personal balance. This is what I have been able to obtain in my life, and I am honoured to be able to share this with you here.

As a verb, balance is to establish equal or appropriate proportions of elements, such as in balancing work and family life. But these are not the only 2 components of you, your life or your being. There are many components to your daily life, and being able to achieve a balance between them all can at times seem impossible.

I shared with you in Chapter 1 how your body is so remarkable that it is able to adapt to whatever environment that you provide for it, but I have also learned first-hand that there is a finite limit to how much adaptation it can undergo. It is not limitless, and it will let you know when you are too close to the tipping point and balance has been lost.

What often happens is you just do not listen to the early signals and do not see the warning signs. For me it came to such a point that I had no choice but to listen, and I had to make changes fast! If I had not made big changes, I would not be here today for my husband, for our children, for my family, or for you.

I ask you now to take a moment and think about your daily life. What does a typical day look like for you? Do you already know that there are some things that you would like to change? Do you feel like you are on automatic pilot and just going through the motions, trying to keep up? Is there never enough time in the day for you to be able to take care of your never ending to-do list?

I know that there was a time in my life when I did not have balance, and it almost cost me my life. I was overworked physically, stretched beyond my capabilities mentally, completely overwhelmed emotionally with my dad's illness and hospitalization as well as being a mom for a third time, and I felt like I had to support everyone else around me. The problem was that I was not supporting myself. This was my near fatal mistake.

Perhaps you too find yourself at times to be in complete overwhelm and exhaustion from living a life that is so jam-packed and out-of-control. Like me, you may find yourself not enjoying the level of health that you desire, and this may seem to prevent you from living a fulfilled life. There is hope, and you too can elevate your life.

I have experienced how easy it is for life to become derailed in what seems like an instant, and because I have been given a second chance I have now dedicated my life to helping you to create a life you love, just as I have in mine.

Creating balance in my life, my family and my business did not come quickly or easily, and I experienced many false starts along the way.

Let's now take the next step, and delve into the topic of finding this balance which at times seems to be so elusive.

2- Finding Balance

Ahh, finding balance. This can seem so easy in theory, but when it comes to putting it into practice, as the saying goes, "Life just seems to get in the way." And I have experienced exactly this. When life is getting in the way of you living your best life, your balanced life, there is truly something wrong.

As I shared with you earlier, there was a time in my life when I did not have any balance, and my body certainly let me know this. It was this experience that led me on a journey resulting in years of studying, research, implementation, and not without trial and error, which led to even more research. The fruits of this labour are the steps that I follow to this day, and am sharing with you.

Finding balance in my life was not easy, but it truly changed everything, from how I interact with my husband, to the fun that we have with our children, to how I relate to my patients, as well as to the time that I cherish to spend with my friends. The biggest shift came when I began to incorporate "Me time." There never used to be such a thing in my life, and this was a contributing factor to my loss of balance.

I have come to learn that as I shifted my priorities and got myself to the top of my own priority list, I was able to establish "Me time." But the shift had to come first.

Do you take any time for you each day? Have you thought about taking time for you? Do you feel guilty just thinking about it, let alone doing it? That is exactly how I felt. I felt that with so much going on in my life and with so many people depending on me, how on earth could I possibly take time away from them when they needed me? The result was not a pretty picture!

There are many different aspects to you, your being, and your life. Some of the things that are packaged here may include: yourself (remember that you and I are shifting you to the top of your list!), and your family. It also includes the things that you do such as: your work, your obligations, your friends, and your recreational activities. Now let's not forget the commitments that you may have made, which may include responsibilities to your neighbourhood community, your spiritual community, your clubs and organizations. And of course other areas of your life that need attention are the health of your physical being, your emotional being, your creativity and personal development, your spiritual being, your relationships, your finances, and your career and vocation. There may also be some other things in your life that I have not touched on in this list, so be sure to add what you want to or subtract anything that does not resonate with you.

Did you notice that I just said "add what you *want* to"? I did not say "add what you *need* to." Do you realize the difference between want and need? The difference truly is huge. I ask you to think on this for a moment because this was a vital concept that was extremely freeing for me. In the course of your day, when you are making choices and decisions, how often are they dictated by your *wants* rather than by what you perceive to be the *needs of others*? I can tell you that my fulfillment with life, and my happiness, shifted greatly when I was fulfilling my wants, what I wanted to do and what truly filled my heart, rather than doing all the things that I perceived that others needed me to do. Talk about a huge amount of completely unnecessary pressure that I was placing on myself. Can you identify with me here? Now trust me when I say that this was not a quick realization, and I had to muster up some courage in order to take the first step towards changing my ways, but with each step I needed less courage, and I felt more empowered every time I made a new choice about how I spent my precious time.

Now let's get to you, and what you want to enjoy in your life. From the list that you compiled from the suggestions above, now comes the challenge. How on earth do you fit it all in, please everyone, as well as add one more thing to the list, that being "Me time?" The first thing I did was take a step back for a moment and breathe. This is a huge shift, and with any change it can be scary. "Oh my! What will others think?" This was the first thing and the biggest thing I let go of. Once you have completed "Heal Your Health," in the back I will provide some resources and a few key books which helped me let go of that mindset.

In regard to shifting priorities, it is important to take stock of how much time you do have available outside of your firm commitments. My firm commitments, or as I refer to them in The Plan (as discussed later in this chapter) as *hard entries*, include: 8 hours of sleep per night, my morning meditation, exercise and journalling routine, my meal times, my office hours, and my commitments to my family. Once these items have been accounted for, you can then calculate the amount of time you have available to do other things.

Here is the math breakdown. There are some constants that never change, and I encourage you to have a go at this yourself as it can be a real eye-opener.

There are 24 hours/day x 7 days/week = 168 hours in a week. 168 hours per week minus (8 hours sleep/night x 7 nights) equals 112 wakeful hours in a week. 112 wakeful hours minus 39 office hours equals for me 73 non-working wakeful hours in a week. Now with my shift in priorities and putting myself at the top of my priority list in order to create balance in my life, I have included my "Me time" as a hard entry in my Plan. My "Me time" includes things like self-care, meditation, exercise, creative time, and relaxation time in order to nourish my body, my mind and my spirit. 73 non-working wakeful hours in a week minus 27 Me time hours/week = 46 wakeful hours that I can share with others in ways that I choose, in order to fulfill my passions and desires for this world. Take some time now and look into what your weekly schedule looks like. I have included my Weekly Plan from the CLEAN™ Living Formula here on the next page for you as an example.

These are the steps that I use in order to ensure balance in my life, clarity in my mind, health in my body, and peace in my spirit, and this is how I have gained balance in every aspect of my life. If you would like to explore this beyond the scope of this book, I invite you to view The Balanced Living Academy™ at http://BalancedLivingAcademy.com, and I can show you how you can do it too.

Have fun with it and take the time to take care of you first.

Dr. Stacey Cooper's Weekly Plan
from the CLEAN™ Living Formula

	Monday	Tuesday	Wednesday	Thursday	Friday	Saturday	Sunday
5:30	Stretch/ Gratitude	Stretch/ Gratitude	Stretch/ Gratitude	Stretch/ Gratitude	Stretch/ Gratitude	Stretch/ Gratitude	Stretch/ Gratitude
6am	Walk Dogs	Walk Dogs	Workout/Eat	Walk Dogs	Weight Training	Walk Dog	Visioning
7am	Get Ready	Get Ready	Walk Dogs	Get Ready	Walk Dogs	Get Ready	Walk Dogs
8am	for Day	for Day	Do my Laundry	for Day	Wash Bedding	for Day	Time with Friends
9am	Office 9-6	Office 9-4	Client Call	Office 9-6 Calls/email	Client Call	Office 9-12	Family Breakfast
10am	Calls/ Email	calls/email Adjustmen	Time w Dean	Chiro Adjustment	Time at Barn	Office	Riding Horses
11am	Office	Office	Reiki Session	Office	Time with Dean	Office	Time with Dean
12pm	Lunch	Lunch	Lunch	Lunch	Lunch	Bank/ errands	Lunch
1pm	Office	Office	Make Supper	Office	Client call	Accounta bility Call	Groceries
2pm	Office	Office	Horseback Riding	Office	Make supper	Riding Horses	
3pm	Office	Office	Client Call	Office	Massage	Riding Horses	1:1 with one of the 4 kids
4pm	Office	Running	Time with Friends	Office	Time with Friends		
5pm	Dinner	Family Dinner	Family Dinner	Office	Kayla Home from School	Family Dinner	Boys Hockey Game
6pm	Yoga-7:30	Time at Barn	1:1 with one of the 4 kids	Family Dinner	Family Dinner	Family Time	Family Dinner
7pm		Hockey Practice				Family Time	My Soccer League
8pm	Read	Read	Read	Read	Read	Read	Read
9pm	Visioning	Visioning	Visioning	Visioning	Visioning	Visioning	Visioning
10pm	Sleep	Sleep	Sleep	Sleep	Sleep	Sleep	Sleep

3-Steps For Cleaning Out Your Cupboards

I have shared with you a lot of information in regards to how to fuel your engine well, so that it may function effectively and efficiently. Because of the importance of fuelling your body well, I feel that the first 1/2 of the workout is to take place in the kitchen. When you take a moment to think of some of the things in your kitchen, do you feel that, from what you have already learned, there is a little tidying up that you could do in your cupboards?

I have found that a key component to ridding yourself of unwanted, needless calories and junk food is that if you do not buy the junk in the first place and it is not in your house, you cannot eat it at 9 o'clock at night. The trouble is that right now I bet that you can think of at least a few things that are lurking in your own cupboards which are sabotaging your health goals.

Can you see that there are already some slight adjustments that you know you can already make when you take your next trip out for groceries?

I have shared a lot about how to fuel your body, and now that you know what to be on the lookout for, it will be so easy to identify those items in the store which will sabotage your health goals. Now I suggest that when you are in the store and you see these items that you will now envision a big red 'X" on the front of them in your mind's eye, so they will not make their way into your cart. This is how you will transform what it is that does come home, and what you are now going to provide for you and your family in order to enjoy enhanced vitality and better body function.

Now let's review some of the things to be on the lookout for. The first thing to do is to identify all the things that your body cannot digest. Remember that your body can only digest foods of the earth. Now is the time to rid your cupboards of chemicals, toxins, preservatives, additives, and anything processed. It is also the time to ensure that any of those kinds of things do not come into your house. This is where the benefit of the Healthy Shopping Blueprint™ comes in. This is the grocery list which only has good healthy fuels on it. When you go to the grocery store you have your purchases already planned out, and this helps to decrease the incidence of those nasty products that are sabotaging your healthy living goals from getting into your cart. Of course the grocery list is the perfect companion to the Healthy Fuels Cookbook™. If it is not on the list then leave it in the store!

You can receive the Healthy Shopping Blueprint™ for free by simply emailing me at drstacey@drstaceycooper.com, subject: Grocery List. You can then place the list conveniently in your home. We keep ours on the fridge door. When you run out of something at home you just have to mark it on the list. When it comes time to go get groceries, then just grab the list and go. It saves so much time and effort when you no longer have to spend time rooting around in your cupboards trying to figure out what you need to shop for.

Continue reading, as in the next section I share with you even more tips on how to create more time in your day.

4-The Benefits Of Learning "The Plan"

I expect that for the most part, when you hop in your car you will have a destination in mind. Certainly it is fun sometimes to just hop in and drive, but that is not the way to efficiently arrive at your goal or destination. In order to ensure that you reach your desired destination, it is important to have a roadmap or a guide. Having a plan in place is a fantastic strategy in order to be able to achieve your desired results, no matter what your goals are.

I am now going to share with you the structure that I have in place in my life, and how I have been able to enhance my health naturally, without having to rely on diets or will power. You can do this too. Here is where you will experience a transformation in your energy levels, your body, and your vitality.

One of your first questions may be "Why do I need a plan?" Sometimes it is fun to take a trip without an agenda and just see where you end up, but if you have a desired destination then do you not plan the trip? The route? The means of transportation? The itinerary? Does this not make it easier to decide on what to pack? The most efficient way to get from where you are now to where you want to be is to have a plan!

I am going to share with you the 5 steps to a healthier you naturally. In Chapter 3 I shared with you the foundation as to what your body needs. How you fuel your engine determines how your engine will run. In Chapter 6 I discussed how certain foods can take you closer to your goals while other foods will only take you further away from your goals. One thing you may not realize is that vibrant health and balance in your body, mind and spirit does not solely revolve around what foods you eat. Even if you feed your body well 100% of the time, if other areas of your life are stressed, your body still will not function well. If you are stressed and you are not sleeping well, or you are not exercising well, you may feel that you have great nutrition but the other areas of your life will still not function as well as they should. Implementing the Plan is important, because this way you will know where you are going, and you will also have the steps in place to know how you are going to get there. It is your roadmap. Once this has been devised, everything else falls into place.

I would like to share with you the importance of what I call "hard entries" and "soft entries" in your calendar. Hard entries would include such commitments as your work hours, while soft entries would be things which are more flexible, like shopping. Utilizing hard and soft entries is my safeguard to ensure that there is not an area of life which gets neglected. If your life is balanced, your body can function optimally.

When I review a calendar for my clients, I help them to ensure that they incorporate strategies in order to be able to create balance throughout the day, while also reducing stress levels by being able to create time for themselves. How would you like to be able to create some time? Yes you heard correctly, 'create some time.' Life can get so busy at times, and of course it is the priorities which get taken care of first. When you are at the bottom of the list, or worse yet, not even on your own priority list, you are not taking care of yourself. As I shared with you in Chapter 2, no one else will do it for you.

When you change your priorities and place yourself at the top of your list, everything will fall into place.

5-How To Exercise Effectively

This next step will be sure to get you moving, as I jump into not just exercise, but how to exercise effectively. There are many health benefits to physical exercise, ranging from improving your cardiovascular health, to strengthening your muscles and therefore your skeleton, to increasing your stamina and endurance, to lowering your stress levels and stimulating your brain and nervous system. However, just as not all foods are created equal and not all drinks are created equal, this also holds true for physical activity. As I discussed in Chapters 11 and 12, there are many different forms of exercise, and not all forms suit every person to the same degree. Let's discover the physical activities that you actually enjoy doing. The importance of this is that the reward cascade, that I discussed in Chapter 4, is also at play here. Research has shown that, when you participate in an activity that you enjoy, this is in and of itself the reward. Two groups of people were utilized in order to demonstrate this effect. Both groups were instructed to complete a walking trail outdoors. They gathered in a reception room once they were finished. In the reception room there was a buffet laid out with many different kinds of food, and the participants were able to help themselves to as much as they liked.

Group A was given the instructions that a trail had been marked out for them, that they were to go and enjoy their walk and the scenery, and that they would all meet in the reception hall at the end for some refreshments.

Group B was given the instructions that for the purpose of exercise a 2 km trail had been marked out for them. This was the same length as the trail for group A. Once they completed the 2 km distance they would meet at the reception hall for some refreshments.

The participants in group B, through the instructions they were given, viewed the task as a job to be completed rather than an activity to be enjoyed.

The participants in group A received enjoyment and pleasure merely from taking a walk on the trail outdoors.

Once both groups gathered in the reception hall after their 2km excursion and they were provided with the buffet table, the servings that they dished up for themselves were measured before they consumed them. Can you guess which group helped themselves to the greater quantity of food and calories from the buffet? What reason did you have for the basis of your answer? Here is what was determined from this study. Those from group B who viewed the physical activity as being a 'chore' or a 'job' consumed the greatest quantity of food from the buffet. The reason is that the buffet was viewed as the 'reward' for completing the chore. The participants from group A, who enjoyed the scenery and the pleasures of spending time outdoors while on the trail, viewed this as being reward enough. Group A consumed much less from the buffet table.

If you recall from Chapter 4, one of the reasons that diets don't work is due to the reward cascade. Remember how I mentioned that cheat days are built right in to a diet because when you work really hard and try to stick to the diet and eat the stupid salads all week, because of all of your hard work, you feel like you deserve a reward? Hence the cheat day. The same holds true for exercise. If you do not enjoy the physical activity that you are participating in, you are already sabotaging your workout efforts. This is exactly what was shown in the study.

In order for your exercise to be effective and actually help you attain your fitness goals, it is important not to sabotage your efforts. My recommendation for effective exercise is to first be sure to select an activity that you enjoy. This way you will not be looking to reward yourself after you have completed the activity. If you hate jogging then do not decide to jog because you have already set up your first roadblock to success. Be sure to choose something that you like, whether it be swimming, a zumba class, rock climbing, playing hockey, walking, playing soccer, running with your dog, cycling, or whatever. The list is very long so just pick what you like, that way you will enjoy it, look forward to doing it and you will then actually want to exercise. Now the reward is built right in.

You may find exercise to be much more enjoyable when you share it with a friend. Spending time with a friend while exercising will not only help the time to go by faster, as you will have someone to talk with, but it is also a fabulous way to incorporate accountability. Often the best made plans can fall by the wayside for many different reasons when you are left to your own devices. At times the list of excuses, as to why not to go for your workout, can be as long as your arm. When you have someone else relying on you to go with them, you are much less likely to let them down. Therefore making a commitment not only to yourself, but to a friend as well, will help to ensure your success rate in attending your workouts, as you will hold each other accountable for your actions.

Another suggestion is to try something new. By learning a new activity you are not only exercising your body and your muscles, but you are exercising your brain too. This will actually use more energy, and will also strengthen the neurological pathways and help to stave off neurological degeneration.

What will you do today to get your body moving? Whatever you choose, have fun!

6-The Importance Of Attitude

Attitude goes a long way in determining longevity. It has been shown that when you accentuate the positive and come from a place of gratitude there is actually a physiological change in your being. To demonstrate this I would like you to participate in this visioning exercise with me. First I ask that you read through this passage and then take a moment to envision what I have described, and then reflect on what you feel. I would like you to imagine yourself in your happy place. I will pick a deserted beach with the nice warm sun shining, a gentle breeze caressing my skin, a gull calling on the wind as it flies by, the sound of the waves gently lapping up on the shore, and the smell of the moist air as I slowly breathe it in. I am grounded, I am relaxed, I am happy, and I am at peace. As I take a nice relaxing breath, I imagine that I am the only person on the beach. There are no distractions. I am alone on the beach but do not feel alone. I just feel peaceful and restful. I ask that you now create that kind of space for yourself in your mind's eye. Go to your happy place and now close your eyes and see your vision in your mind's eye, and take a few minutes to settle in.

After you entered your quiet place and rested there for a moment or two, did you check in to see how you were feeling? If you forgot, don't worry, you can do that now. Take a moment and realize how you felt when you were in your happy place. What feelings came over you? Did you notice a shift in your stress level? Did your blood pressure change? Notice your heart rate. Did your breathing change? Generally you may find this scenario to be relaxing and soothing. Were you able to relax? Did you feel your breath slow down as you relaxed? Nothing happened to you physically on the outside, but inside your physiology did change.

As you recall from Chapter 1 how your body adapts to every environment that you provide, your physiology also changes when your body gets stressed. Whether it is emotional stress, or stress at work, or of life in general, if you are stressing your system, it cannot function optimally.

When you shift your attitude in a positive direction, this will enable you to change how you perceive the stressors around you. This alone will go a long way in reducing overall stress levels.

It is important to focus your attention on these concepts which will propel you forward, not backwards, and which allow for accentuation of the positive. This will enable you to enjoy a life filled with gratitude and happiness, and will not only affect your health outcomes but will also open up so many other opportunities and experiences which you may not have become aware of with a pessimistic attitude.

Are you ready for a transformation in your life? Perhaps you are tired of being tired and not living your life to the fullest. Do you realize that it is you who is in control of your outcomes? Do you now know that there is hope? Are you ready to learn how to live your life with better body function and optimal health? I have been fortunate in that I was given a second chance, and you know that I have since dedicated my life to helping you create balance and optimal health in your life. I want to support you. My gift to you, with love, is to help you to uncover what your next best steps are. I ask you to receive this free gift for yourself by simply emailing me at drstacey@drstaceycooper.com with subject: Gift, and let's develop your next best steps together.

Change is hard on your own. When you have the motivation but not the direction or the correct information, even with the best of intentions it is very difficult to do it alone. Very seldom is success self-taught. Learning is the key to expanding your horizons, to broadening your vision, and realizing your goals. Together we will set the stage for your success by developing your next best steps. We will create strategies to rejuvenate your mind, your body, and your spirit. You will be able to explore different methods which will enhance your outlook, and you will be able to nurture yourself so that you can be the best you with enhanced vitally, a greater love for life, and for those around you.

If I had not listened to my body during my crisis and had not changed my life, I am certain that I would not be here today. Just imagine yourself having the energy to be able to play with your children or grandchildren instead of only being able to sit in a chair and tell them a story. How much money will you save by starting now and reducing your dependence on prescribed medication, chronic health interventions, visits to the medical doctor, and hospital stays? What do you want your outcome to be? You do have a choice.

Being able to live a balanced life truly enables you to change perspective about everything. In this chapter I discussed attitude, and this is a key to unlocking the door to a whole new you. When you make a shift to a positive outlook and begin to put yourself on your own priority list, and take the steps to work "The Plan," you can handle anything that comes your way. I am speaking from experience. I invite you to read on and see how I was able to make lemonade from the lemons I was given.

When, If Not Now?

Record Your W.I.N.N.s Here

_____

_____

_____

_____

_____

_____

_____

_____

_____

_____

_____

_____

_____

_____

_____

_____

_____

_____

_____

_____

_____

Chapter 15

Making Lemonade

Life is 10% what happens to you
and 90% how you react to it.
— Charles R. Swindoll

The day was Mother's Day, Sunday, May 12, 2014. It was a glorious, sunny spring day. The sky was so blue, and there were no leaves on the trees yet as winter was just barely over. As was our tradition, I was served breakfast in bed with all of our kids, and it truly seemed like a regular Mother's Day. None of us had any idea what lay in store for me that day, and as I reflect back on it, it turned out to be one of the most wonderful days of my life.

At this point we need to backtrack just a little bit. On April 4, 2014, my husband Dean and I attended a conference in Akron, Ohio, where I met my soon-to-be mentors Noah and Babette St. John. During the course of Noah's three-day workshop, it was my husband who gave me the gentle nudge forward to expand my horizons, to create more offerings for my patients, and to have a greater reach within the health and wellness community. After some very careful and deep consideration, not to mention apprehension on my part, we took the HUGE leap and I signed up for a full comprehensive coaching program so that I could up-level and create an online business alongside my chiropractic practice. This decision was not made lightly, as it also came with a large financial investment. Our children were still quite young and at home, and to commit to such an endeavour along with the financial commitment at times weighed heavily on my shoulders. Everything rested with me, and it would be only me to blame if it failed and the money was 'wasted.' I was very excited for the opportunity and ready for the challenge of creating something new. My Baba lived to be 93 years old and she always said "As long as you learn something new each day, then you can take the rest of the day off!" Taking this new avenue into a world of the unknown and that of the World Wide Web, and seeing what could come of it, was a wonderful challenge. Something you need to know at this moment is that for us living out in the country our internet service was practically non-existent. We were still on dial-up, and the only thing I used the internet for was for emails in regards to soccer practices or hockey games. I did not do anything online, I did not surf the web, and I didn't even have a laptop. So needless to say I did not have a clue as to what I was getting into.

After having made this huge financial commitment, we were so fresh into it that I had not even had my first coaching call yet, and now Mother's Day was upon us.

We have four children, and living out in the country we have always instilled the responsibility of chores and helping out in the family. And this is not only because work needs to be done, but it is also because we are in the process of raising responsible young adults who are respectful of themselves and their own space. We are teaching them to be able to look after themselves when they are on their own. It is very important for me to know they can take care of themselves. Just as an example, they have always made their school lunches since starting kindergarten. They always come grocery shopping so they can learn how to make healthy choices, and each of them has a dinner night when they prepare meals for the family. There is always a weekly rotation of chores within the home, which includes cleaning bathrooms and floors, and they all do their own laundry. When they go out on their own, I am not going to be there with each of them to take care of this for them so it is our responsibility as parents to teach them how to do it for themselves.

Living in Canada, I am proud to say that we are rink rats. All of us have spent many hours at the arena during our lifetime. Our oldest figure skated while our other 3 play hockey. As you know, this is not free, so it is also important for us to teach them the value of the dollar. We live in the bush and heat with wood. And this is one of the chores that the children are involved in. We explained to them that if they did not want to do wood then we could heat with oil, but then there would not be the funds to pay for all of their hockey. That was a very quick end to that discussion because of their deep desire to participate in their extracurricular activities. As it is said, "A family that works and plays together sticks together."

So on this Mother's Day it was my request that we spend an hour in the bush doing wood. I love being outside and in nature, and listening to the birds in the trees, the breeze blowing, the sun on my face, and connecting with mother Earth. It was a very productive morning, and once everyone had finished up I decided that since I was dirty anyway, and it was such a beautiful day, I would continue splitting wood, for it is something that I truly enjoy doing, just like mucking out the stalls at the barn with the horses. Our neighbour Paul was in the bush with me, cutting wood.

Everything was going along wonderfully until I felt pressure on my right index finger. Of course it was me who was running the controls of the wood splitter. With the remarkable reaction time of the nervous system, it enabled me to sense the pressure in my right index finger, process that information and decide that I needed to let go of the controls with my left hand. This all happened within such a short timeframe that part of my finger was still left intact and was not completely severed off. I am still in awe of this.

Over the years Paul and I have spent many times together working in the bush. I called to get his attention as I was now trapped in the wood splitter. He knew that I would not be calling to him, with the chainsaw running, unless I really needed him. He shut the saw off, came over to me, and shut off the engine to the splitter. I said to him "I'm stuck! Grab that piece of wood off the ground and knock this one off the wedge to get me free." As my hand was released I raised it and took my glove off to see what had happened. As I was holding my hand up and I saw the backdrop of the glorious blue sky and the bare branches of the spring trees, what I noticed was how snow white the bone of my finger was. Luckily it was still attached on the bottom side. We grabbed some paper towel from the quad and started to make our way back to the house. I told Paul that my purse was in the Excursion, and the keys were in it and he could drive me to the hospital. Our youngest son Jake was just making his way out to come and help some more. I called out to him and said, "I have pinched my finger. Would you please go get the ice pack from the basement freezer?"   Having the ice pack was important, but it was also a diversion tactic as I really did not want to traumatize any of the kids with the sight of my finger, as I was not even sure at that point as to what the outcome of this might be.

As we made our way to the emergency room and my husband Dean was able to come and meet us there, I had time to contemplate my new situation. Here is where I had a choice. I could choose to accept this tragedy and receive it as a tragedy. I could choose to place my entire self-worth in my profession and my livelihood. As a Doctor of Chiropractic your hands are a crucial component of your services. At that moment I could choose to decide that my hand was forever damaged, that my career was over, that my livelihood was finished, that my earning potential was zero, and that my life was over as I knew it.

I chose differently.

As I was sitting in the hospital, the first thing I considered was to determine how vital this particular finger was to my adjusting technique, and for my livelihood, and my life. I knew just by looking at it that, even if the finger was reattached, there would be 8 to 12 weeks for bone healing, there could be reconstructive surgery, and there would be rehabilitation and physiotherapy. This was not going to be a quick fix. So I decided in those moments that if it turned out at the finger was not going to be worth much in the end anyway, just lop it off, stitch it up, and I would be back to work in a few weeks. Luckily this is not how it turned out.

After all of the examinations, X-rays, and multiple phone consultations with the reconstructive surgeon and the emergency room doctor, it was determined that the finger was salvageable. My husband said "For heaven sakes, it's a finger, at least give it a chance!!" As it turned out, even though the finger was partially severed I still had full movement of the joints at the distal end of my finger because the tendons were still intact. Remarkably, I also had full sensation and motor control as none of the nerves were severed. Basically the wood splitter just cut the bone. When I contemplate this, how on earth does a wood splitter miss all of the tendons, ligaments and nerves in a tiny little finger?? My answer is fate!

Fate provided me the opportunity to step away from my practice, to have a locum come into my office to take care of my patients, and to enable me to dedicate four full months of my life to healing, resting, and creating. This provided a huge expansion to my creative side because now I had to retrain my brain. I had to learn how to write left-handed, I typed one-handed, and I had to develop brand new concepts as well as go through a huge learning curve in regard to all things related to the workings of the World Wide Web. Timing is everything. I dedicated my time to creating my brand new business, Lifestyle Balance Solutions™, my online Health and Wellness Lifestyle program the Balanced Living Academy™ and creating my Healthy Fuels Cookbook™.

Through the course of my healing I remarkably gained full and complete function of my injured finger. I have full feeling right to the tip of my finger, and I have zero cold intolerance, which is really important because we still spend so much time in the arena watching the kids play hockey, and I now play hockey too. There is not anything that I cannot do with my hands.

I have come to understand that it was fate on that Mother's Day. And if it hadn't been the wood splitter it would have been something else. I would have fallen off my horse and broken my leg or something. I was meant to be at my kitchen table for those four months, to be able to create a life that I love.

I chose to grow and expand through adversity, and I chose to make lemonade from the lemons that showed up for me on that Mother's Day, as much for myself but also as a model for my children in living a life that matters!

When, If Not Now?

Record Your W.I.N.N.s Here

_____
_____
_____
_____
_____
_____
_____
_____
_____
_____
_____
_____
_____
_____
_____
_____
_____
_____
_____
_____
_____
_____

Chapter 16

A Life That Matters - Author Unknown

The only limits to the possibilities in your life tomorrow are the buts you use today.
— Les Brown

A Life That Matters
Author Unknown

Ready or not, some day it will all come to an end.
There will be no more sunrises, no minutes, hours, days.
All the things you collected, whether treasured or forgotten,
will pass to someone else.
Your wealth, fame and temporal power will shrivel to irrelevance.
It will not matter what you owned or what you were owed.
Your grudges, resentments, frustrations, and jealousies
will finally disappear.
So, too, your hopes, ambitions, plans, and to-do lists will expire.
The wins and losses that once seemed so important will fade away.
It won't matter where you came from,
or on what side of the tracks you lived.
At the end, whether you were beautiful or brilliant, male or female,
even your skin colour won't matter.
So what will matter? How will the value of your days be measured?
What will matter is not what you bought, but what you built;
not what you got, but what you gave.

What will matter is not your success, but your significance.
What will matter is not what you learned, but what you taught.
What will matter is every act of integrity, compassion, courage or
sacrifice that enriched, empowered or encouraged others.
What will matter is not your competence, but your character.
What will matter is not how many people you knew, but how many
will feel a lasting loss when you're gone.
What will matter is not your memories,
but the memories that live in those who loved you.
Living a life that matters doesn't happen by accident.
It's not a matter of circumstance, but of choice.
Choose to live a life that matters.

Afterword

This is not the end of your journey, as it is just getting started. This journey continues, just as a circle does. There is no break, no beginning, no ending, just a continuous evolution of you becoming your best you. With each new day and every choice you make, you are continuously providing an environment for your body. As you begin to choose differently, your body will adapt to your new environment and you will see change.

With the knowledge that you now possess, all of the power is in your hands. When your highest priority shifts to become that to Heal Your Health, the only thing left to do is to choose. I have laid out here for you in this book many choices. Now be sure to hear this! It is not my expectation and definitely not my intention for you to implement all of these tools all at once, for this will surely guarantee failure. You may wonder why I would tell you this. I ask you now to recall the importance of baby steps, to start with where you are starting from, and to set attainable goals to strive for. Attempting to implement all of these choices all at once can create frustration and disappointment, and you could decide that none of it works, and you will quit.

This absolutely works, and I am living proof! One of the reasons why diets do not work is due to frustration. Frustration and disappointment are two key components to failure. When you begin to make lifestyle choices which are obtainable and realistic and in a positive direction, results will become evident quickly, and this will spur you on to continue your journey to optimal health. Just start with a single step, as this is all that it takes to begin.

It is with deep gratitude that I thank you for welcoming me to walk with you on your journey to a healthy lifestyle. Here is to Healing Your Health Naturally!

With much love,
Dr. Stacey

If not now, when?

Laugh Loud, Love Large, Live Life!
— Dr. Stacey Cooper

ALSO BY DR. STACEY COOPER

Dr. Stacey Cooper's Healthy Fuels Cookbook™
Fuelling Your Body For Enhanced Vitality Naturally
Wheat, Gluten, Dairy, Soy and Sugar Free Recipes
that your whole family will love

International Best Seller
What's Self-Love Got To Do With It?
How 14 women learned to love themselves.
Compiled with Heather Andrews

25 Awesome People I Know
with Sarah Pass and Friends

DR. STACEY'S MISSION

My mission is to eliminate the Type 2 Diabetic Epidemic Globally through my non-profit W.I.N.N. Foundation.

W.I.N.N. is my acronym for **When, If Not Now!**

Scientific research is indicating today that this is the first generation of children who's life expectancy will be shorter than that of their parents. As a society we are going backwards instead of progressing in regards to health related issues.

Food manufacturers are producing artificial food substances which are creating many diseases. The preventative disease, of most significant consequence, is that of childhood obesity which directly leads to adolescent onset Type 2 Diabetes.

The outcomes from these diseases are life altering and devastating. Elevated blood sugar levels can affect various cells and organs in the body. Complications from Type 2 Diabetes include: kidney damage, often leading to dialysis; eye damage, which could result in blindness; an increased risk for heart disease or stroke; a decreased ability to heal from wounds and sores, which leads to amputation of limbs. These outcomes are life altering and this degenerative disease process is reversible.

As you have learned throughout this book there are many things that you can do right now to begin to heal your health naturally and reverse these degenerative disease processes. You can turn around your health outcomes by changing the environment that you provide for your body.

It is my mission to share this with the world so that others may know that they too can change their outcomes and that there is HOPE!

If you or someone you know has been touched by this, I encourage you to join me in my mission. Email me at drstaceycooper@gmail.com and lets WINN this together.

ABOUT DR. STACEY COOPER

Dr. Stacey Cooper is an inspirational keynote speaker, presenter, Doctor of Chiropractic, educator, entrepreneur, wife and mother. She is also the founder of Lifestyle Balance Solutions™, host of #AskDrStacey Monthly Mentor, Award Winning Author of Heal Your Health, International Bestselling Author of What's Self-Love Got To Do With It?, creator of the Heal Your Health Blueprint™, the Balanced Living Academy™ and author of the Healthy Fuels Cookbook™.

What led Dr. Stacey to initially create Lifestyle Balance Solutions™ was in immediate response to suffering her own health crisis as a result of not having balance in her life. She was unaware of the extent of her strength or what this life-altering experience would uncover for her and her family.

Dr. Stacey's 'rediscovery' of what it takes to be healthy in this crazy world, and her journey to the realization of a deeper relationship with herself and her family, led her to ultimately find the way to balancing her life and restoring her health.

Along with Dr. Stacey's clinical experience which spans over 23 years, she has now created online products as well as personal mentorship programs for her patients and clients.

With her own chiropractic practice which spans 4 generations, (her great-grandfather started the practice in 1912) and success stories of her patients and clients, Dr. Stacey has been featured in many different media outlets: Business Innovators Radio on iHeart Radio, and Business Innovators Magazine with Mark Stephen Pooler, FiveD TV Eye on Life with Dr. Lana Marconi, radio interviews on the Beth Bell Radio Show on iHeart Radio, Living Regret Free with Dr. Gayle Carson, Light on Living with Lisa Berry on Om Times Radio, and The Heather Andrews Show.

As a speaker, Dr. Stacey inspires audiences by sharing her story, her discoveries and the strategies that continue to help her optimize her health and well-being. Being an advocate in self-discovery, self-love and revitalization, she is making a positive difference.

Her purpose is to help enable you to enjoy your years with enhanced vitality and better body function. Dr. Stacey's mission through her non-profit W.I.N.N. Foundation is to eliminate the Type 2 Diabetic Epidemic Globally. To join Dr. Stacey simply email her. Receive Dr. Stacey's FREE Training *How to Eliminate Your 5 Hidden Energy Drainers* at www.DrStaceyCooper.com.

Find Dr. Stacey online:
Website: www.DrStacey360.com
Facebook: https://www.facebook.com/DrStaceysNation/
Contact: drstacey@drstaceycooper.com

Resources

Balance Your Life and Enjoy Enhanced Vitality & Better Body Function!

Unhappy with the lack of results you are getting from diets and weight loss schemes? Learn how my clients are getting healthy, feeling better and losing weight while enjoying an improved quality of life!

- Quickly become empowered in order to make the right choices for enhanced health
- Incorporate balance into your daily routines
- Reduce stress in your life for improved quality of life
- Engage techniques for quieting the mind and the body

Join Balanced Living Academy™ now at BalancedLivingAcademy.com

How To Have Improved Health, Wellness and Enhanced Vitality Quickly and Easily!

The Healthy Eating Blueprint™ is an easy to follow and easy to implement series which enables you to enhance your vitality. The essence of this series is to allow you to eliminate those things which are robbing you of your stamina and draining your energy.

- Gain more energy than you have had in years
- Fast and easy ways to eliminate things from your life which are draining your vitality.
- This is the way to better body function and healthy weight loss naturally!

Get the Healthy Eating Blueprint™ Now at HealthyEatingBlueprint.com

What's Self-Love Got To Do With It?
How 14 women learned to love themselves.

What's self-love got to do with it? The answer is—well, *everything*! The love and worth you have for yourself sets the foundation for the types of relationships you have. What you believe is what will be achievable in your life. Your self-love and worth will help you to hold yourself accountable in your life, business, and career.

Read how 14 women learned to love themselves, how they set themselves free, so they could dream bigger and be a better human for themselves and for others. Learn how they created better revenue streams after hitting rock bottom so they could rebuild their lives and help serve others.

Each chapter is followed by lessons from the author, mindset tips to help you grow, and space for journaling your thoughts.

You are not alone here. Join us on the discovery to loving yourself.

For your own personally autographed soft cover copy of *What's Self-Love Got To Do With It*? simply contact Dr. Stacey directly via email at drstacey@drstaceycooper.com to arrange delivery. Or simply grab your copy of the E-Book right here at
https://drstaceycooper.com/self-love-book/

Find Dr. Stacey online:
Facebook: https://www.facebook.com/DrStaceysNation/
Complimentary Consultation:
support@lifestylebalancesolutions.com
Subject Line: SELF-LOVE

Dr. Stacey Cooper's
Healthy Fuels Cookbook™

I have created this cookbook to enable you to fuel your body well with nourishing breakfasts, hearty meals and delicious desserts, because what is life without dessert? It is all about balance!

Food is a necessity for life on a daily basis and great nutrition is easier than you think. Get your copy now and see how easy it is to experience better body function.

We are a busy family of 6 and know that mealtimes can get hectic. All of the recipes in my cookbook have been tested by my family. They are easy to follow and have been approved by ALL of the members of my family. My husband Dean and our four children enjoy making these recipes and especially enjoy devouring the end products. I always figure, "What good is it to have a recipe if the kids don't like it and won't eat it?", so you will not find any of those kinds of recipes in my *Healthy Fuels Cookbook™*!

To order your full colour, coil bound copy of the Healthy Fuels Cookbook™, simply email me at drstacey@drstaceycooper.com with Subject Line: Cookbook and we can make arrangements for pick up at my office, or for delivery.

For a full colour PDF version of the cookbook simply go to http://www.drstaceycooper.com/healthy-fuels-cookbook/ and place your order and receive immediate delivery to your email inbox.